THE NATURE OF ULTIMATE REALITY AND HOW IT CAN TRANSFORM OUR WORLD:

Evidence from Modern Physics; Wisdom of YODA

THE NATURE OF ULTIMATE REALITY AND HOW IT CAN TRANSFORM OUR WORLD:

Evidence from Modern Physics; Wisdom of YODA

Pradeep B. Deshpande, PhD
*Professor Emeritus of Chemical Engineering
University of Louisville,
Visiting Professor of Management
University of Kentucky, Lexington, Kentucky,
President and CEO, Six Sigma & Advanced Controls, Inc.*

James P. Kowall, MD, PhD
*Independent Researcher
Eugene, Oregon*

Copyright © 2015 by Six Sigma & Advanced Controls, Inc.

Six Sigma & Advanced Controls, Inc.
P. O. Box 22664
Louisville, KY 40252-0664 USA.

All rights reserved. Except for appropriate use in critical reviews or works of scholarship, the reproduction or use of this work in any form or by any electronic, mechanical or other means now known or hereafter invented, including photocopying and recording, and in any information storage and retrieval system, including electronic transmission, is forbidden without the written permission of the publisher.

ISBN 13: 978-0-9651639-9-6

Library of Congress Control Number: 2014917993

Disclaimer

The material in this book is meant to be of an instructional nature. Consult your physician or healthcare professional before engaging in any of the practices outlined herein. The book is sold with the express understanding that the purchaser assumes full responsibilities for any or all health, financial or other liabilities arising out of its use.

Dedicated To

Baba
Shivanand Ji

Sadhguru Jaggi
Vasudev

Maharishi
Mahesh Yogi

Sri Sri
Ravi Shankar

Baba Ramdev

Mikel Harry

Konstantin
Korotkov

W. A.
Tiller

Rollin
McCraty

David R.
Hawking

Roger
Nelson

Huping Hu and
Maoxin Wu

Gregg
Braden

If you wish to understand the universe, think of energy, frequency, vibrations - Nikola Tesla
(Seated left of Swami Vivekananda)

What you seek is so near you that there is no space for a way.
I am That: Talks with Sri Nisargadatta Maharaj, 2nd Ed., Acorn Press, Durham, NC 2012
(With Permission from the Acorn Press)

Foreword

This monograph is all about excellence. It holds a promise and is based on the premise that excellence, both internal and external, is the way forward towards a state of perfection. Every human being is born with some intrinsic qualities - an initial state of his excellence, in accordance with his /her actions and deeds of the past, and has an opportunity in the present to evolve to a new and hopefully better state of excellence through his actions and deeds in the present. He or she continues this march on the staircase of excellence, sometimes in a non-conscious way and at other times more consciously. Meditation is the conscious way of refining the excellence of the internal through positive impact on internal energetic, thoughts, the process of thinking, emotions, intentions, focus and level of concentration, desires, attitudes, intellect, ego, enthusiasm, sensitivity to disturbances, and level of consciousness etc.

The process of meditation sharpens these nonmaterial, non-physical forces and aids in revealing the domain of the unmanifested truth or reality, generally unavailable unless in a state of contemplation. These nonmaterial objects are too complex to describe and have virtually infinite shades and degrees of fineness or coarseness. Thus for instance, emotions can be of various types such as sensuality, anger, greed, possession, attraction, jealousy etc., and these can vary in their intensities and refinement. Broadly speaking they can have a positive or negative impact on the extent of excellence achieved. Similar situations exist with all other internal forces. A positive outlook and a sense of being right for the individual and the rest of the surroundings around him is thus essential for the rise. Meditation, contemplation, comprehension help to curb the negatives in favor of positive, a stage necessary for higher levels of internal excellence.

This monograph is attempting to tell us something about internal excellence. These nonmaterial nonphysical objects are all within us and form the seed that manifests as material and physical objects of the external. The internal and external are thus connected in an almost mysterious way. Through several scientific examples the monograph brings forth this connection and appeals to modern science to unravel the details of the mechanism and the role of this connectivity. It promises that once on an external, that is, material and physical platform, the modern science has all the tools and understanding and structured methodology such as six sigma to achieve external excellence.

At present, there are no ways of directly measuring internal excellence on any monitor. However, their reflections or variations in their intensities and magnitudes can be indirectly picked up on a device called gas discharge visualization unit that captures the bioenergy field of humans and other objects. This is a significant development as described in the book and will go a long way in realizing the connection of the internal with the external.

A substantial part of the monograph is devoted to consciousness. This is again a very complex object to describe and varying in shades depending on its level. At the physical level, it may simply mean being alert to know what is around us, but as we progress on the scale of excellence, it can ultimately go to a level of pure consciousness connecting the microcosm to the macrocosm. A beautiful simile in arithmetic terms can describe it to some extent. We take unity (one) as a symbol of completeness, perfection and finality. This unity however can be represented in several ways and can have different meanings: For instance:

$0^0 = 1$ — Nirgun, Nirakar, pure consciousness, without quality attributes and form, Advaita-without the second, primordial soup, the Absolute

$1^0 = 1$ — Sagun, Nirakar, pure consciousness, with quality attributes but no form

$1^1 = 1$ — Sagun, sakar, pure consciousness, with quality attributes and form

$\sqrt{1} = \pm 1$ — Maya, illusion, multiplicity of forms, duality

$\sqrt[3]{1} = \pm 1$ — Three real roots or one real root & two imaginary roots; three quality attributes S, R T components described in the book

$\sqrt[5]{1} = \pm 1$ — Shabda, sparsha, roopa, ras, gandha – the five senses

$\sqrt[8]{1} = \pm 1$ — Ego, intellect, mind, ether, air, water, fire, earth

And so on. These are all children of unity (the same value everywhere) and hence of pure consciousness in their variety and attributes. The authors describe in their own style the meaning of consciousness and its implications on the rise and decline of individuals, nations and cultures. They also fractionate consciousness into its Satvic (s), Rajasic (R) and Tamasic (T) components and describe ways to measure them and alter them to achieve higher levels of consciousness and the bio-energetic fields. The implications of these on the health and wellness, achieving exemplary performance, global peace and nonviolence are presented through examples.

The main message of the monograph is that the entwining of the internal and external, like in the strand of a DNA, is the only way to achieve total excellence. The book is written in a simple lucid style and is compelling, thought provoking, and enjoyable.

Dr. B. D. Kulkarni
Distinguished Scientist (Engineering Sciences),
CSIR Distinguished Professor and Dean, AcSIR
CSIR-National Chemical Laboratory, Pashan road,
Pune 411 008 India

Acknowledgments

The image on the front cover is an Aura photograph of my Guruji, Guru Mahan Maharishi Paranjothiar (www.universalpeacefoundation.org) taken by an Icelandic lady while Guruji was visiting Iceland. On a subsequent occasion, the team of four from Iceland visited Guruji's Ashram at Thirumoorthi Hill, Tamil Nadu, India in the year 2000. This time, the Aura-capturing video camera on a tripod captured the Aura (light) emanating from Guruji going to the team. The reader might keep this citation in mind while reading the book. Avdhoot Baba Shivanand Ji is another self-realized yogi in Delhi who has developed a program for materialization of intentions which he refers to as Science beyond Science. These two yogis are like two peas in a pod, only that one delivers his wisdom in Tamil while the other in Hindi but we know language hardly matters because the medium of communication is emotions not speech. A beautiful example of this is the experience of the visiting team from Iceland. They spoke only Icelandic, not English, forget about Tamil. After they took the Aura photograph and saw the image, they cried like a baby and not out of sadness.

There are other self-realized yogis in India too. Among them are Swami Ramdev, Sadhguru Jaggi Vasudev, and Sri Sri Ravi Shankar. The late Maharishi Mahesh Yogi pioneered the Transcendental Meditation program. The late Dr. David R. Hawking was an eminent psychiatrist and the author of Power vs. Force and the Map of Consciousness.

There are several other individuals I wish to extend grateful thanks to, not in any particular order. Dr. Mikel Harry, currently CEO of Six Sigma Management Institute, is the Co-Creator six sigma at Motorola in the seventies along with Bill Smith. He has taught six sigma to a large number of Fortune 500 CEOs over the years. Dr. Konstantin Korotkov, Professor of Biophysics at St. Petersburg Federal University of Information Technologies, Mechanics, and Optics, is the Creator of Gas Discharge Visualization devices to capture the bioenergy fields of humans and other objects. It is remarkable that he and his associates were able to tie the ancient knowledge of the Chinese energy meridians and the Indian chakra system to the physiological, psychoemotional and consciousness states of a human. The GDV has been approved by the Russian health authorities for use as a medical diagnostic device in Russia. Dr. W. A. "Bill" Tiller is Professor Emeritus and former Head of the Department of Materials Science and Engineering, Stanford University. He is the creator of Psychoenergetic Science. Dr. Roger Nelson, Princeton University directs the Global Consciousness Project while Dr. Rollin McCraty directs the Global Coherence Initiative at the Institute for HeartMath. Dr. Huping Hu, PhD (Biophysics, University of Illinois), JD (New York Law School) is a practicing attorney in New York and is married to Dr. Maoxin Wu, MD (Shanxi Medicine College China), PhD (University of Illinois). Dr. Wu is Professor of Pathology and Director of Cytopathology at Mount Sinai School of Medicine in New York. Drs. Hu and Wu are coeditors of the Journal of Consciousness Exploration and Research. Gregg Braden is the New York Time best-selling author of the book

The Divine Matrix. In their own way all of these individuals are on a quest to better humanity.

Thanks are due to Dr. Bhaskar D. Kulkarni, PhD for writing the Foreword and also for several decades of cooperative R & D. Grateful appreciation is extended to Sanjeev S. Aroskar, B. Tech. Electronics and Computers, IIT Bombay, for years of cooperation and teaching the first author the wherewithal of Nirguna Sadhana and Saguna Sadhana. Grateful thanks are also due to Sanskrit & Ayurveda scholar Dr. S. N. Bhavsar in Pune for assistance in translating the various Sanskrit sutras and shlokas into English. The helpful discussions with Dr. Rollin McCraty, Head of Research at the Institute of HeartMath are gratefully acknowledged. The cooperation of Krishna Madappa in Taos, New Mexico is gratefully acknowledged. Special thanks are due to Tony Belak, Ombudsman at the University of Louisville for partnering with me in our quest to introduce these ideas at the University of Louisville. I extend grateful thanks to Dr. Rebecca Martin and Dr. Walter E. Dibble, Jr. for their cooperation.

I thank Sam Rangaswamy, Acharya Prakash Pokhrel, Babu Sharma, Pradeep J. Mehta, Avinash L. Kelkar, Raja Ananthakrishnan, Senthil Anand, Vasant B. Waikar, Kunwar Bhatnagar, Paul Foreman, and Yogesh Pardeshi for cooperation. I thank my long-time friend and former colleague W. L. S. Laukhuf for the editorial help. Thanks are also due to former students, friends, and associates who took the time to write a blurb for the book.

Pradeep B. Deshpande
30 October 2014

PREFACE

I will soon be 72 but this story begins in July of 1972 when I had just returned to India after my graduate studies at the University of Alabama and Arkansas and had joined the faculty of Chemical Engineering as an Assistant Professor at the Indian Institute of Technology, Kanpur. Soon thereafter, India's Finance Minister Mr. Y. B. Chavan, paid a visit to the campus and talked to the Institute faculty imploring them to do something significant for the development of India. IIT-Kanpur was one of five premiere institutes of engineering and technology in India and as such we were expected to make national contributions and not just teach some of the brightest young minds in India who hardly needed us to teach them. I was sitting in the back row with colleagues and dear friends to this day, Dr. D. Ramkrishna, now a Chair Professor of Chemical Engineering at Purdue University and a member of the National Academy of Engineering and Dr. Arvind P. Kudchadker, recently retired as Founder- President of a private University in India, wondering how someone like us working in a narrow and highly specialized field like Chemical Engineering could possibly do something for the development of a nation. But the idea stuck in my mind for some reason. I returned to the US after spending an academic year at Kanpur but have visited India annually ever since. On one of these visits soon after I had joined the faculty of Chemical Engineering of the University of Louisville in 1975, I read an intriguing headline in the Times of India: "India will be a super power by the turn of the century". Again, I wondered, how a beggar nation which was importing food under the PL-480 food-for-peace program of the

United States, could possibly become a super power in a short span of twenty-five years. But, the idea stuck in my mind anyway.

Fast forward to July 1985 and I had just become Chair of Chemical Engineering at the University of Louisville. I was conducting research in advanced process control and optimization searching for technologies for achieving perfection. On Mondays, Wednesdays, and Fridays my colleague and dear friend, The Late Phoebus M. Christopher and I would drive off-campus for lunch. Being of Greek ancestry he too had bit of a philosophical streak in him. We would discuss myriad of topics, some interesting and others mundane but among them was one that resonated deeply with us both: Rise and Decline of Cultures. For reasons that weren't entirely clear, I would argue that the rise and decline of societies was inevitable and he would say, may be so, but where was the scientific evidence other than the historical observation that great cultures of the past, including his own, Greece, had all eventually declined. Of course, he was right.

One day on our usual lunch break, we decided if the phenomenon of rise and decline was real, we ought to be able to find the evidence of it in the Encyclopedia Britannica. Being a reputed western source of reference, we decided we would focus on Greece. I was getting ready to go to India in the summer of 1991 on my usual annual visit when Phoebus said by the time I got back he would have a list of every person born in Greece included in the reference. I nodded telling him that was a great idea but really didn't think anything was going to come out of it; After all, there were twenty-three volumes of the Encyclopedia Britannica at the time. I got back to Louisville in August and on the first day back to my office before the classes began for the fall semester, I heard a knock on my office door. Phoebus came in and a tossed a bar graph across my table and my jaws dropped. The data clearly showed the rise and decline of Greece! Greece has remained dear to me ever since. I have been going to Athens as a visiting professor to conduct a two-week six sigma course in the MBA program of the University of Kentucky at TEI/Piraeus in Athens for the past nine years in a row and I don't intend to quit as long as my health permits and University of Kentucky lets me.

With the Greek data at hand, we decided to investigate three more nations: Great Britain, Germany, and the United States with the help of graduate students Sandeep Dronawat and Bharat Sanghvi to find out if the evidence of rise and decline was evident for these countries as well and it turned out that it was. In 1993, I wrote the self-published article with Phoebus "On the Cyclical Nature of Excellence". We had the paper reviewed by several eminent persons including Dr. Donald W. Swain, President, University of Louisville; Professor Rutherford Aris, Professor of Chemical Engineering, University of Minnesota, a member of the US National Academy of Engineering, and others. They all agreed, the use of the Encyclopedia for the evidence of rise and decline was unique but that to rely on a single reference source no matter how reputable was problematic. We respected their view but remained convinced about the soundness of our findings. Ensuing years added strength to our conviction.

By 1994 I had learned that the concept of rise and decline was mentioned in the Bhagvad Geeta. I must have read the

Geeta umpteenth number of times that year and finally it all became clear: human beings have three components of the mindset, S, R, and T. This has been true in the past and will remain so in the future unless nature itself decides to change its own natural laws. Societies rise and decline because the three components undergo transformation over time. The precise reason for this remains unclear. Increasing S component induces the society to rise and when it reaches the peak, the T component begins its ascent and the society begins to decline and it continues to decline until the T component cannot reduce anymore and the S component gains prominence and the society begins to rise again. These ideas and the performance of Indian-Americans and Chinese-Americans in this country led me to offer a theory of rise and decline of societies in the mid-nineties predicting the imminent rise of China and India in that order when no one was talking about it. Rise and decline are extremely slow phenomena but the ensuing years have proved the predictions to be correct. My own PhD students scoffed at the idea in the nineties but at my retirement dinner in 2005 hosted by the department with the help of my friend and former PhD scholar Dr. Kenneth W. Leffew, Research fellow at DuPont, some of them came up to the stage to say they withdraw their reservations.

By the turn of the century I had guided nearly twenty doctoral and forty master's scholars and wrote nearly one hundred papers in the field of advanced process control and optimization. These scholars had developed several control technologies for achieving perfection. Then I heard about six sigma from my longtime friend Sohan L. Makker with whom I had gone to graduate school at the University of Arkansas. He told me that General Electric, his employer, was making lots of money because of six sigma. He was happily telling me how GE employees were getting bonuses which in some instances exceeded their annual salaries. This news was disconcerting since I thought we had understood the limits of perfection and how to achieve the best possible performance; how could there be something better? That prompted me to study six sigma in depth buying book after book on the subject only to realize that we weren't missing anything. We had never considered applying our knowhow to service processes. With this realization, I reconsidered process control concepts, meshing them with six sigma principles and subsequently developed a unifying framework for six sigma and process control. With this framework, it was possible to assert that six sigma could be applied to any process or transaction be it static or dynamic, linear or nonlinear, manufacturing or service. Six sigma was not just another quality initiative but rather a way of life meaning we should live the six sigma way. I traveled to Scottsdale, Arizona in the year 2000 with friend and associate Bill Fowle formerly of Colgate-Palmolive Co., for a meeting with Dr. Mikel Harry, cocreator of six sigma. I will always cherish Mikel's comment, 'What you have done is unique and revolutionary'. I subsequently began teaching a graduate course in six sigma in the Chemical Engineering Department which was attended by students in virtually every engineering discipline and the course was always oversubscribed. In 2005 I signed up for phased retirement to fully retire by December 2008. During this period I also introduced a two-week mandatory Six Sigma Green Belt training program in the new MBA curriculum of the Gatton College of Business & Economics, University of Kentucky, a course I continue to teach in their

MBA program in Greece. These offerings were one of the first six sigma offerings in higher education in the world. Subsequently, I was given the opportunity by the Private University Council, Ministry of Higher Education, State of Kuwait to train Kuwait higher education professors and management staff in six sigma principles in a year-long program. The group did exceptionally well and at the end of that assignment, I teamed with my dear friend and eminent educator Prof. Imad M. Alatiqi, then Secretary General, PUC, and presented a talk on How to Transform Higher Education with Six Sigma at the conference of International Network of Quality Assessment Agencies in Higher Education in Abu Dhabi in March 2009.

During this time, I wrote a monograph, A Small Step for Man: Zero to Infinity with Six Sigma the foreword and introduction to which were written by Dr. Dipak C. Jain, Dean of the Kellogg School of Management, Northwestern University, and Dr. James C. Watters, Chair of the Chemical Engineering Department at the University of Louisville, respectively. Both expressed a sense of disappointment that the theory of rise and decline appeared to leave no scope for human intervention; we were just helpless witnesses to the debacle as our societies declined. Actually, the phenomenon of rise and decline applies to societies at large not to individuals, placing no limit whatsoever on individuals in any society in whatever phase of rise and decline to rise to the maximum extent possible for a human being. Furthermore, as this book will show, it is possible to delay the decline of risen cultures such as the United States, accelerate the rise of emerging cultures such as India, and change the direction of cultures currently in the state of decline.

Parallel to these research areas, I was fortunate to have come across the programs of several yogis some of whom spoke the language of science including six sigma. It became clear they had the recipe for transformation, i. e., how to raise our S component, and they were presenting the knowhow on national TV programs in India to tens of thousands of viewers. But they had no theory to back up the valuable practices. Over time, I learned the intricacies of their yoga programs and experientially benefited from them. However, as an engineering educator I knew their way of teaching just wasn't going to work with the rational minded. Then I came to know about the path-breaking book, The Divine Matrix by the NY Times best-selling author Gregg Braden, a computer scientist. In his book, Gregg presented several fascinating experiments of outstanding western scientists who were searching for something within us which could have an impact on ourselves. Several renowned scientists including Max Planck, Albert Einstein, Nikola Tesla, and others had come tantalizing close to unraveling the mystery but couldn't quite connect the dots because in this instance the teacher and the student is one and the same. The path-breaking work of Nobel Laureates Watson and Crick on human DNA changed that. It became possible to study how something within ourselves can affect ourselves, our DNA, because we could locate it outside our bodies, somewhere else. On the basis of these experiments these scientists concluded that something which has an impact on ourselves is emotions. Positive emotions induce life-supporting changes while negative emotions, life-degrading changes. Now, the yogic programs could be put to the test with experimentation. With this understanding, a scientific framework for individual transformation to raise the S component was at hand and it was possible to assess progress with a six sigma project.

Even with all this, a scientific measurement device to gage our S, R, T level of consciousness was sorely needed. Konstantin Korotkov's path-breaking work on gas discharge visualization came to the rescue. Over fifteen years ago, he developed a device to measure the bioenergy field of humans. As it turns out, the bioenergy field is capable of revealing the physiological state, psychoemotional level, and in some cases consciousness of subjects. The device is registered by the Russian health authorities as a routine medical diagnostic device for use in hospitals and doctor's offices.

But could we bring about societal changes or are we destined to serve only as witnesses, helplessly observing as societies rise and decline. It turns out that we need not. A few years ago I became aware of the work of some Princeton researchers. The researchers discovered, on the basis of some one hundred electronic random number generators located in the various part of the planet, that collective human consciousness becomes aware of impending major events well before the events themselves occur. One example they present is the 9/11 event. OK, but how does merely observing calamities help? This is where ancient yogic wisdom and the work of the Late Maharishi Mahesh Yogi becomes important. He passed away in 2008. He had many world renowned scientists and celebrities as followers, among them quantum physicist John Hagelin, The Beatles, film maker David Lynch, comedian Jerry Seinfeld, television host Merv Griffin, among a host of others. There is a full-fledged University named after him in Fairfield, Iowa. Maharishi showed that a limited number of people of meditators can bring about changes not only within themselves but in the society around them. He proved the concept in Washington DC showing how a limited number of meditators were able to reduce major crime in the capital. Maharishi is not with us anymore but Yoga Guru Baba Shivanand Ji is attracting tens of thousands to his yoga programs which also yield similar results. I too have experienced the benefits of Pranayam- Yogic breathing pranic exercises, and meditation. It is heartening that prestigious publications such as Nature, Science, Proceedings of the National Science Academy-US, Forbes, Archives of Internal Medicine, NeurologyNow, and others have carried full-length articles on the myriad of benefits of meditation.

In the context of the theory of rise and decline what all this means is while the rise and decline of societies is inevitable, it is possible to delay the decline of developed nations such as the United States, accelerate the rise of emerging nations such as India, and change the direction of nations currently in decline such as Greece. Arguably for the first time in history a scientific framework for world transformation and peace is now available. Now it should be clear why I keep going back to Greece to introduce the knowhow of transformation there. Greece isn't going to be a developed nation any time soon for the rise and decline is a slow phenomenon taking hundreds of years to play out. However, it should be possible to bring about the winds of change in short order.

Until recently I had taken six sigma to be the ultimate in achievable performance believing that it alone was sufficient to transform emerging nations into developed nations. A couple of years ago sitting in a business-class lounge at

Heathrow Airport Terminal 5, reading an article in the Financial Times, it suddenly hit me that it wasn't so. The elephant in the room was the level of internal excellence, the level of consciousness (The strength of the S component). In other words, in the absence of adequate internal excellence, six sigma programs will lead to suboptimal performance. There is strong evidence to support this hypothesis. Dr. Harry and I have written a column, Criticality of Internal Excellence in Six Sigma for National Transformation, to spread the word. Two years ago, I introduced the science of internal excellence in the six sigma course in the MBA program in Greece, taught it last year for the second time and will teach it again in the forthcoming program in February 2015 and the students love it.

The world has become increasingly rational minded over the course of the last two thousand years or so and that is not a bad thing. But it also means that the more scientific the framework is, the better are the chances the world will embrace it. I have been presenting a lecture on the scientific framework for internal and external transformation in various countries; five to date: USA, India, Congress of Peru at Lima, Greece, and Russia. I presented a lecture on this topic at the 17th Annual Conference on Science, Information, and Consciousness in St. Petersburg, Russia in July 2013.

In the context of this book, the work of Biochemist Elizabeth Blackburn assumes importance. She discovered in the seventies that a high level of stress reduces telomere length and lowers telomerase enzyme levels and accelerates aging. A variety of serious ailments including cancer are caused by high stress levels. The American Medical Association says stress causes 80% of the diseases. This work earned Professor Blackburn the 2009 Nobel Prize in Physiology and Medicine. The GDV investigations have shown that high level of stress disrupts our bioenergy field and throws chakras off-balance. Blackburn has shown that meditation lengthens telomeres, raises telomerase levels and reverses aging. The GDV investigators have shown that meditation has a restorative effect on the bioenergy field and the state of the chakras. The advantage of GDV over the telomere approach is that the former does not require the analysis of blood samples costing upwards of $500 per sample.

Finally, on the title of the book, THE NATURE OF ULTIMATE REALITY AND HOW IT CAN TRANSFORM OUR WORLD. The yoga programs referenced above as well as the evidence presented in the book Divine Matrix suggest that our consciousness remains connected to the universal consciousness just as it was at the moment of the Big Bang moment. It is as though the mystery of life unraveled in the discussion so far and the mystery of the universe are intricately linked. In this connection, I am fortunate to have come to know coauthor Jim Kowall in recent years. Jim kept insisting that I read Amada Gefter's book, Trespassing on Einstein's Lawn and I am glad I listened. Amada began her quest to unravel the mystery of the beginning of the Universe in 1995 when she was barely fifteen. Her path-breaking book gives a fascinating account of how this rebellious Jewish teenager from New York with the guidance of her beloved father Warren Gefter and with the help of world-renowned physicists including John Archibald Wheeler, Stephen Hawking, and others figured out the mystery of the beginning of the universe leading her to reach the mind-blowing conclusion, *"The ultimate reality, that which remains after everything else in the Universe has vanished, is the nothingness of the void"*. Coauthor Jim Kowall himself is an eminent theoretical physicist turned medical doctor and with the inspiration of a self-realized yogi Nisarga Datta, the author of the classic "I Am That", reached an equally mind-blowing conclusion, "The nature of Nothingness, the void, cannot be anything else but consciousness, cosmic consciousness to be more precise". The scientific framework already knows that individual consciousness and the cosmic consciousness are intricately linked. In fact our individual consciousness is a microcosm of the cosmic consciousness. Reflect on how everything was connected to everything else at the moment of the Big Bang event when the universe was the size of the Planck Length (10^{-33} cm in diameter) and the experimental evidence on how we remain connected to one another, then you will appreciate it.

Although this book has been inspired by the challenge posed by the Finance Minister of India in the early seventies, the underlying wisdom belongs to ancient treasures of humanity including Vedas, Upanishads, Geeta, Yoga, and many seers, past and present who include self-realized yogis, world renowned scientists, and the pioneers of six sigma.

The chapters in the book are organized in a logical manner for ease of reading and comprehension and not in a chronological order. The book shows the pathway for individual, organizational, national, and global transformation and peace and along the way illustrates how it will lead to great health, exemplary performance in all walks of life including business performance, less discord and violence, interfaith understanding, racial harmony, foreign policy guidance, and a host of other benefits. My text, Six Sigma for Karma Capitalism, 2011, together with this book can serve as texts in a course on internal and external excellence which ought to be a required course in college curricula. It appears that the challenge posed by the Indian Finance Minister has been met, and then some.

Pradeep B. Deshpande

Contents

Dedications v
Foreword vii
Acknowledgments xi
Preface xv
Contents xxix
Mystery of the Universe xxxiii
Mystery of Life xxxv
CHAPTER 1. How It All Began 1
CHAPTER 2. How We Got Here 5
CHAPTER 3. Theory of Rise and Decline 9
CHAPTER 4. The Ultimate Reality and Nature of Consciousness 15
CHAPTER 5. Who Am I 33
5.1 Adaptation of Baba Shivanand Ji's Discourses 34
5.2 Modern Physics Perspective 38
CHAPTER 6. The Two Domains of Excellence 45
6.1 Domain of the Manifest 45
6.2 Atmanic Consciousness and S, R, T Level of Consciousness 49
CHAPTER 7. How to Measure Consciousness 53
7.1 Scale of Consciousness 54
7.2 How to Measure the Level of Consciousness 56
7.3 The Brahma Uncertainty Principle 60
7.4 Simpler Way to Measure LOC 62
7.5 Assessing the Strength of the Principle 64
7.6 Underlying Principle 67

7.7 Outcome Measures of LOC 67
CHAPTER 8. Bioenergy Field Measurements......... 71
8.1 Principles of Gas Discharge Visualization 72
8.2 Computational Algorithms in Bio-Well.................... 74
8.3 Chakras and Interpretation. 74
8.4 Normal Energy Ranges 78
8.5 Working with GDV Device 79
CHAPTER 9. Discovering something within ourselves that can affect us 85
9.1 Field of Energy that Affects our DNA...................... 86
9.2 Everything is Connected to Everything Else 88
9.3 Effect of Emotions of DNA 90
9.4 Effect of Coherence + Intentions on DNA 91
9.5 Effect of Emotions on Others...........................92
CHAPTER 10. Why We Get Sick 95
10.1 Yogic Perspective...95
10.2 Nobel Laureate's Breakthrough Work................100
10.3 Quantum Mechanical Perspective.....................103
10.4 Changes in Atomic Configuration? An Example....122
CHAPTER 11. How to Raise our Consciousness 129
11.1 Conscious Approach..130
11.2 Process to Raise the S Component....................130
11.3 Evidence..133
11.4 Roots of Meditation...138
CHAPTER 12. Pranayam...141
12.1 Swami Ramdev's Pranayam Program.................142
12.2 How Pranayam Improves Health......................144
12.3 Case Study Louisville Pranayam Group..............145
CHAPTER 13. Meditation for Materialization of Intentions..149
13.1 Six Sigma Project-Materialization of Intentions....156
13.2 Select Yoga Sutras...159
13.3 The Practice..163

13.4 The Results..165
CHAPTER 14. Why Six Sigma............................171
CHAPTER 15. Criticality of Internal Excellence in Six Sigma Programs..177
15.1 Internal Excellence Boosts Business Performance..178
15.2 Mumbai's Dabbawallas..................................179
15.2 Kumbh Mela..181
15.3 Gamarra Businesses of Peru..........................184
CHAPTER 16. Collective Consciousness for World Peace...187
CHAPTER 17 Interfaith Understanding and Racial harmony..197
17.1 Interfaith Understanding...............................197
17.2 Racial Harmony..200
17.3 Nuclear Weapons..200
17.4 Is Democracy Right for Everyone....................200
CHAPTER 18 Science and Spirituality: A Perfect Stand-off..203
APPENDIX I Supplementary Information...............245
A. Publications on Meditation...............................245
B. Famous Personalities Who Meditate...................246
C. Solicited Feedback from Friends and Associates.....248
Biographical Sketch of Authors.............................251

MYSTERY OF THE UNIVERSE
THE NON-PHYSICAL NATURE OF ULTIMATE REALITY: THE SOURCE OF CONSCIOUSNESS

(Source: http://photojournal.jpl.nasa.gov/gallery/universe)

In her path-breaking book, Trespassing on Einstein's Lawn, Journalist Amanda Gefter, who had never taken a course in physics, managed to talk to renowned physicists such as John Archibald Wheeler and others and exchanged emails with Stephen Hawking finally reaching the mind-blowing conclusion: *Nothing is ultimately real.* Her final conclusions are: The ultimate reality is the infinite, unbounded, undifferentiated, primordial nothingness, often called the void. Everything in the world is radically observer-dependent, and the observer's world only emerges when a boundary arises in the midst of this primordial nothingness.

Later in this monograph are presented the equally mind-blowing conclusions: "The *ultimate reality, the primordial nothingness, cannot be anything else but the source of con-*

sciousness", and *"The individual consciousness of an observer, along with everything in the world an observer observes, can only emerge in a bounded, differentiated state of this primordial nothingness"*. In the Vedic tradition, consciousness in its infinite, unbounded, undifferentiated, primordial state can be called *Brahmanic consciousness*, while consciousness in its finite, bounded, differentiated state can be called *Atmanic consciousness*.

Although the world is conventionally thought of as the nature of reality, this understanding of ultimate reality tells us the world is an emergent reality that can only emerge in Atmanic consciousness. Ancients have experientially known this for thousands of years. Rig Veda paradoxically states, '*Not the non-existent existed, nor did the existent existed then.*' (http://en.wikipedia.org/wiki/Nasadiya_Sukta). This ancient wisdom is also expressed in Genesis, in the writings of Plato, and in the Advaita tradition of Shankara. This wisdom also tells us that everything is connected to everything else, that it has been so since the world was created, and will always be so. What we forget is that we remain connected today and forever. The weakening of the link of our individual consciousness with the universal consciousness leads to a myriad of problems. The wherewithal of how to strengthen this link is what this monograph is all about.

THE MYSTERY OF LIFE

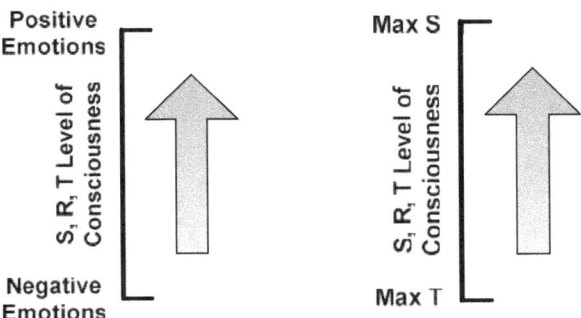

Two Equivalent Representations of Consciousness

It is equally amazing that the mystery of life should turn out to be so simple. It is all about positive emotions (unconditional love, empathy, kindness, compassion), which translates into energy, frequency, vibrations!! The Guru of Baba Shivanand Ji would say to young Baba Ji on self-realization, *Sab Kuch Bhav Hai Re* (It is all about emotions). Nikola Tesla was on the mark too. The feeling of disconnection with the cosmic consciousness occurs due to our ignorance, ego, mind, and the intellect and this leads to all kinds of problems including illnesses, suboptimal performance, discord and violence. This monograph presents the wherewithal of how to overcome this feeling of disconnection for health and wellness, business excellence, national transformation, and global peace.

CHAPTER 1
How It All Began

At the big bang event, there was only a repulsive force, a kind of anti-gravity, called dark energy. In relativity theory, the force of dark energy is understood as a cosmological constant, Λ. There is no explanation in physics for the origin of this force. Observational evidence shows that the "bang" in the big bang is an explosion driven by an accelerated or exponential expansion of space. The two pieces of evidence for this expansion are measurements of the cosmic background radiation supporting the idea of inflationary cosmology and the current observed accelerated expansion of the universe as measured by the accelerated rate at which distant galaxies are moving away from us. The distant galaxies are moving away from us faster the farther out we look as though they repel one another. At the moment of creation, the universe was about a Planck length (10^{-33} centimeter) and its temperature was extremely high as determined by the Hawking temperature equation:

$$kT = \bar{h}c/2\pi R \qquad (1.1)$$

Where

    R is the size of the universe, 10^{-33} centimeter at the moment of creation
    k is the Boltzmann's constant, $1.3806488 \times 10^{-23}$ m^2 kg s^{-2} K^{-1},

$\bar{h} = h/2\pi$, where h is the Planck's constant, $6.62606957 \times 10^{-34}$ m² kg/s,

c is the velocity of light, 299,792,458 m/s

This gives the temperature T of about 10^{32} Kelvin. In relativity theory the radius of the cosmic horizon, R is determined from the value of the cosmological constant, Λ according to

$$(R/\ell)^2 = 3/\Lambda \qquad (1.2)$$

Where

ℓ is the Planck length, and
Λ is the cosmological constant.

For a point of reference, the size of an atom is 10^{-8} cm while that of an atomic nucleus is 10^{-13} cm. Inflationary cosmology hypothesizes that Λ was about 1 at the moment of the big bang event, while the current measured value of Λ is about 10^{-123}. Inflationary cosmology also hypothesizes that Λ reduces in value through a process akin to burning as a state of high potential energy transitions into a state of lower potential energy (mass energy, kinetic energy, potential energy, thermal energy), and as energy burns, heat is radiated away.

To further elaborate, the radius of the cosmic horizon is the size of the observable universe as observed by an observer (a point of reference, not a human observer) at the central point of view. The radius-squared of the cosmic horizon is inversely related to the cosmological constant. The universe only inflates in size from its initial size of about a Planck length to its current size of about 15 billion light-years because dark energy has been burning away and the value of the cosmological constant is decreasing. As dark energy burns away, heat is radiated away in the form of photons of electromagnetic radiation. These very high-energy photons can transform into particle/anti-particle pairs, like electron/positron pairs and proton/anti-proton pairs. The proton is a composite particle of quarks, while the anti-proton is a composite particle of anti-quarks. The transformation occurs according to the standard model of particle physics. Conversion of energy into mass gives birth to galaxies, stars, planets, and other matter. Currently, the observable universe is estimated to comprise of 5% matter, 27% dark matter, and 68% dark energy. The problem of converting energy into mass is called the problem of baryogenesis. For galaxies, planets, stars, and other matter to exist there has to be more matter than anti-matter. The explanation of why there is more matter than anti-matter in the universe is provided by something called the parity violation, which is a kind of symmetry breaking. The weak nuclear force breaks a symmetry called parity. Parity is the symmetry under mirror reflection, and it turns out that the mirror reflection of a neutrino is not the same neutrino, but is much more massive. The result of parity violation is that anti-protons decay into electrons and so in the universe there is predominately matter rather than equal parts matter and anti-matter. This kind of parity violation can only occur due to the very high energies present shortly after the big bang event. As the universe inflates in size and cools, protons become stable and so we are left predominantly with matter. This is how it all began. In the next chapter, we will take it from here and take us to today.

CHAPTER 2
How We Got Here

With this brief overview of inflationary cosmology and particle physics explaining how galaxies, planets, stars, and other matter came into being, let us see how we humans have reached the current stage. Here too, we begin with the Big Bang event except now we follow the Vedic reasoning. The Vedic wisdom suggests that the creation, sustenance and destruction of the universe is a cyclical process, as are all natural processes, meaning that there is no beginning and no end (Brahma creates – Big Bang, Vishnu Sustains, and Shiva Destroys - Big Crunch). In this scenario, the energy present at the moment of the Big Bang comes from the previous, most recent Big Crunch. Stephen Hawking offers an alternate explanation. The universe could expand forever. The critical aspect to remember here for later reference is that everything in the universe was connected to everything else when the universe was the size of the Planck length. Apparently we remain so connected to the present time. Recognition of this wisdom provides many practical benefits.

With galaxies, planets, stars, and other matter in place, the next thing to focus on is a habitable planet, at least as we understand life here on Earth. This being our home, the planet Earth is one we are most familiar with but there is no reason to suppose that ours is the only habitable planet in the universe, or for that matter, our understanding of life is the only one possible. An astonishingly large number of things have to come together to make life possible. For example, distance from the parent star which provides energy required for life, just the right amount of tilt, period of rotation about itself and around the parent star, location of other planets in the system and their relative locations, hospitable atmosphere and the temperature environment, presence of liquid water, are among a host of things we may know little about or fully comprehend.

In the evolutionary scheme of how life evolved here on planet Earth, among what is required first is habitable temperature and liquid water to make life possible. Anthropological evidence suggests that life on Earth began in the form of single-cell organisms. Of course, given all the constituent elements and all the available gadgets, how to create life remains a mystery. Single-cell organisms evolved over time giving birth to multi-cell organisms, to Chimpanzees, and finally to early humans. Anthropologists peg this to have occurred in Africa from where groups of humans emigrated to other parts of the globe possibly in search for better means to support life or may be because of their adventure gene. Some of the early groups appear to have arrived in North Africa, China, and India followed by Europe and the Americas. The Brahma-Vishnu-Mahesh scenario has built into it a theory of human existence. Figure 2.1 shows this cyclical process. In Figure 2.1, the universe is depicted as coming into existence with the Big Bang at B. Now, shifting attention to Earth, life forms at C when

Chapter 2. How We Got Here

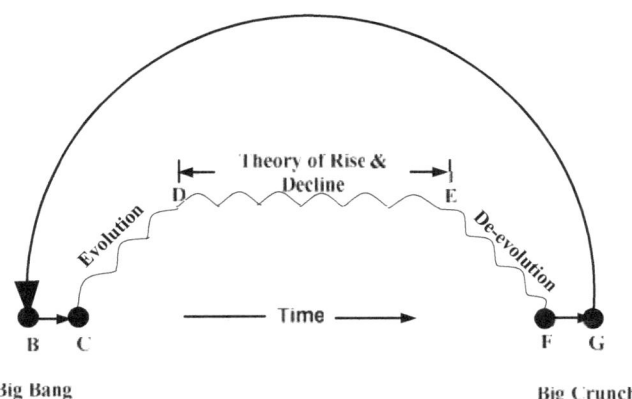

Figure 2.1. The Brahma Vishnu Mahesh Cycle

favorable conditions develop. Appropriate living systems then evolve into human beings as per the theory of evolution at D. Then, the soon-to-be-discussed theory of rise and decline comes in to play between D and E. In Figure 2.1, one particular culture or society, any society, is depicted for illustration. At E, human beings are conjectured to begin evolving to lower life forms until prevailing conditions end all life on Earth at F. Finally, the Big Crunch occurs at G and the universe is withdrawn in favor of the next Big Bang. Between C and F the possibility of an extraterrestrial event (e. g., an asteroid strike) or a terrestrial event (e. g., stupidity of human beings) wiping out much of life on Earth cannot be ruled out. However, in the scheme depicted, life would have to return some time thereafter allowing for the natural cycle to continue. The energy of our Sun is finite and sooner or later, it will be exhausted. Life would have come to an end long before the Big Crunch but in the comforting words of Stephen Hawking, "Don't panic, calamity is not around the corner".

CHAPTER 3
Theory of Rise and Decline

Of practical interest in the Brahma-Vishnu-Mahesh Cycle is what happens between D and E. Vedic wisdom allows us to propose a theory we call, *theory of rise and decline* which posits that while humans continue to evolve into better beings throughout their span of existence, the society where they live will sustain repeated rise and decline over time. Immigration and emigration do change the attributes of the concerned society but unless the numbers are substantial, the attribute of the host society does not change sufficiently enough to escape the effects of rise or decline. We are well aware that great cultures of the past have all risen and fallen. To gather additional evidence, a Greek-American colleague of the first author at the University of Louisville and his doctoral students examined every volume of the *Encyclopedia Britannica* (there were twenty three volumes at the time) in the early nineties and noted the number of persons from specific cultures that were listed. The reasoning behind this exercise was that if a culture indeed sustains rise and decline, the data ought to show it. The Encyclopedia Britannica being a western source of reference, we selected Greece, Great Britain, Germany, and

10 | *Chapter 3. Theory of Rise and Decline*

the United States for scrutiny. Illustrative data for Greece and Great Britain are shown in Figure 3.1.

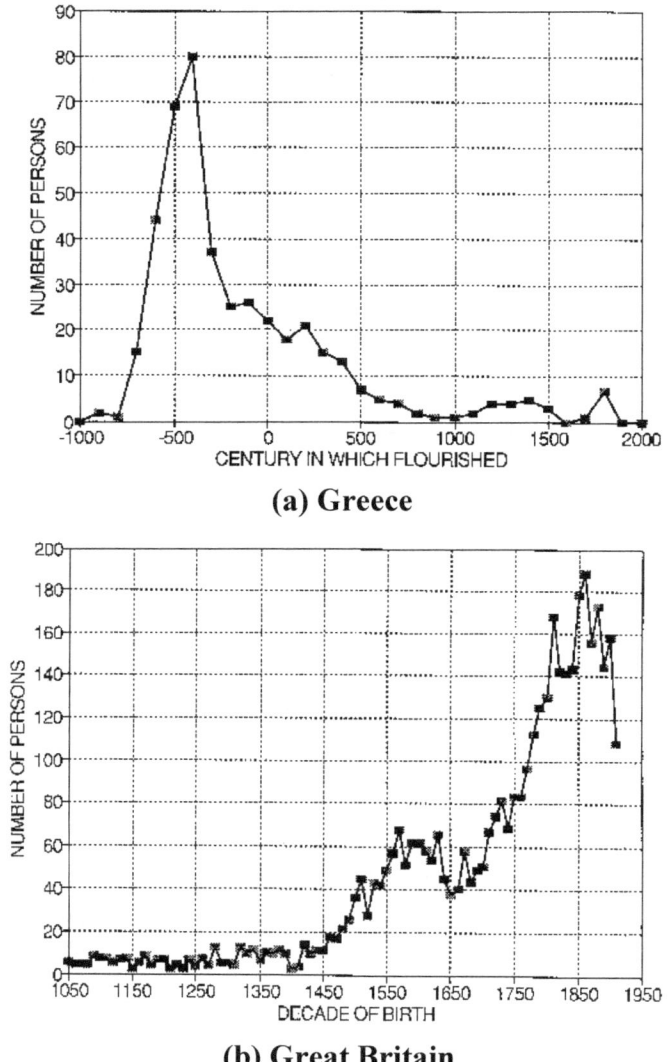

(a) Greece

(b) Great Britain

Figure 3.1. Rise and Decline of Greece and Great Britain

Chapter 3. Theory of Rise and Decline

The rise and decline of these societies is self-evident. Just think where Greece was during its rise and where it is today! The word of Aristotle was God, not subject to debate, even though he might have been wrong on occasion as in the case of his assertion of an Earth-centric nature of our solar system. The first author has been going to Greece for the last nine years to teach six sigma to MBA students of the University of Kentucky at TEI/Piraeus in Athens and has witnessed unmistakable indicators of decline throughout the Greek society. As another example, it used to be said *the Sun never sets on the British Empire* but now it sets there like everywhere else.

This work on rise and decline was reviewed by several eminent individuals including the then President of the University of Louisville, an eminent historian, and a Professor of Chemical Engineering at the University of Minnesota who was a member of the US National Academy of Engineering, among others. These reviewers pointed out that while the use of Encyclopedia Britannica was unique and the data presented interesting, caution ought to be exercised as we were relying on a single source of reference no matter how reputable, to draw broad conclusions. On the flip side, the reason for the confidence is that such a phenomena had been predicted several thousand years ago and the data in the Encyclopedia Britannica is seen to be supporting it. Based on the theory, the first author predicted the imminent rise of China and India in the early nineties when no one was talking about it. His own doctoral students scoffed at the idea at the time but at his retirement dinner with many years of industrial experience working for multinational companies under their belt, they were happy to withdraw their reservations.

Vedic wisdom offers an explanation for why cultures rise and decline but it requires access to the following natural laws:

1. Societies rise and decline as a natural course.
2. The phenomenon of rise and decline is cyclical.
3. Rise and decline of cultures occurs due the transformation of the three components of the mindset.

To explain this natural law, the mindset is taken to have three components:

- ✓ **S Component**: Truthfulness, honesty, steadfastness, equanimity.
- ✓ **R Component**: Attachment, bravery, ego, ambition, greed, desire to live.
- ✓ **T Component**: Lying, cheating, causing injury in word or deeds, sleep

Mathematical proof of a natural law cannot be given. The way to dispose of a natural law is to find evidence to the contrary and none has been forthcoming to this day. Now, assume that the three components of the mindset are fractions summing to 1 and the minimum value of each component required for life is 0.1. This gives the maximum possible value of 0.8 for any of the components. We, the six and a half billion inhabitants of Earth, have varying proportions of these three components that make up who we are. A person of the mindset (0.8, 0.1, 0.1) is the best anyone can be while a person of the mindset (0.1, 0.1, 0.8) is the worst he or she can be. Readers of all faiths, races, and nationalities should be able to identify individuals in both categories from their societies throughout history. The rest of us have these three components in varying proportions between the two extremes. This has been true for thousands of years as it is today, and is independent of the religious faith (if any) of the individual. Some readers might ask a perfectly reasonable question, "If we have evolved from lower life forms to what we are today, why mightn't we evolve to some higher form in the future rendering the present natural law invalid?" The answer of course is, yes, it is possible, but as long as the three components continue to guide human existence, the foregoing concepts will have to remain valid. There must necessarily be science for how and why this transformation occurs. Perhaps someday scientists will decipher it.

The third law asserts that the mindset undergoes transformation over time as a natural course. The influence of environmental factors on the transformation of the mindset cannot be ruled out. During the course of rise, the society's S component gains dominance reaching a high peak when the society is at its best following which decline must ensue and the T component begins its ascent reaching a peak when that society is at its worst and so on. These concepts are further explained in Figure 3.2. There is nothing in these laws to suggest that all nations must rise to the same height in terms of their achievements, nor decline to the same depth in terms of the injury they inflict upon themselves or others.

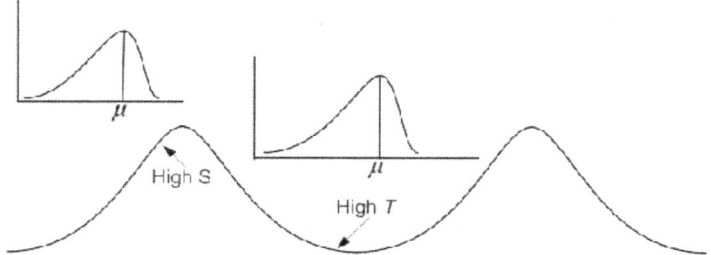

Figure 3.2 Transformation of the Mindset Components Causes Rise and Decline of Societies

Dr. Deepak C. Jain, the then Dean of the Kellogg School of Management, Northwestern University and Dr. James C. Watters, Chair of the Chemical Engineering Department at the University of Louisville in writing the Foreword and Introduction respectively to the monograph, A Small Step for Man: Zero with Infinity with Six Sigma expressed a sense of disappointment commenting, *the theory of rise and decline appears to leave no scope for human intervention.* Actually, the theory of rise and decline applies to societies at large placing no limit on an individual from a society in any phase of rise and decline to rise to the maximum extent possible for a human being. There is ample historical evidence that it is so. In fact, this book will show how to bring about such a transformation and how that can in turn help societies begin to turn things around and make this a more peaceful world.

CHAPTER 4
The Ultimate Reality and Nature of Consciousness

Everything must be based on a simple idea.
Once we have discovered it, it will be so compelling
so beautiful, that we will say to one another,
yes, how it could have been anything different.

John Archibald Wheeler

The ultimate reality is what remains when there is nothing left. Thus, ultimate reality and nothing are closely related. Journalist Amanda Gefter discovered that the answer to the question *what is the ultimate reality* lies in being able to probe the question, *what is nothing* (*No Thing*). This is the question Warren Gefter posed to his teenage daughter, Amanda Gefter in 1995 when they were dining at their favorite Chinese restaurant in Ardmore, Pennsylvania, just west of Philadelphia. *Nothing* can be understood as *the absence of everything, whereas the ultimate* reality can be understood as *that which is uniform, unbounded, undifferentiated, and eternal*. Nothing becomes something only when a boundary arises, like a sandcastle on a beach. In this chapter, we probe this concept further in search of the answer to the question, what is the nature of the ultimate reality. The scrutiny has a direct bearing on the theme of the monograph for individual, organizational, national, and global transformation and peace.

In a previous article Kowall, (2014) made a scientific argument regarding the non-physical nature of ultimate reality as the source of consciousness. This chapter extends the argument in a natural way, but without reliance on any specific aspects of physics. At the end of the chapter these logical conclusions are correlated with the findings of modern physics which have been well documented in the recent book by Amanda Gefter (2014).

The question is about the nature of ultimate reality. We appear to live in the world, but this created world is not the ultimate nature of reality. This created world is an emergent reality that emerges from the ultimate reality. Ultimate reality is not only the source of everything in the world; ultimate reality is the source of the world. There are two related questions: What is the nature of the ultimate reality and how does the world emerge from the ultimate reality? It is remarkable that modern physics provides some answers. Even more remarkable, these scientific answers resonate deeply with the answers given by many of the world's most revered religions.

The first question about the nature of ultimate reality has an answer that we can deduce from logic and reason alone. When we look at the world, we see distinct things. The very distinctness of things implies a boundary that separates each thing from all other things.

Only this boundary defined in space and time allows us to distinguish anything from all other distinct things. Modern cosmology has shown that even the observable world has a distinct boundary beyond which we cannot see anything.

17 | *Chapter 4. The Ultimate Reality and Nature of Consciousness*

This cosmic boundary in space and time is called a cosmic horizon. The remarkable nature of the cosmic horizon is every observer has its own horizon, which is to say the cosmic horizon is observer-dependent.

Every observer is present at the central point of view and the cosmic horizon is a bounding surface of space, like a spherical surface, that surrounds the observer at the central point of view. This discovery of modern cosmology only confirms our observations that all distinct things are defined by a boundary, including the world itself.

The strange aspect of this discovery is that every observer in some sense has its own world delineated by its own boundary in space and time. We can only speak of a consensual reality shared by multiple observers when their individual world-delineating boundaries overlap with each other and in some sense share information.

This is where logic comes into play to help us understand the nature of ultimate reality. Every distinct thing in the world is delineated by a boundary in space and time including the world itself. The ultimate reality is the source of everything in the world including the world itself. Since the ultimate reality is the source of everything, and everything is defined by a boundary, the ultimate reality itself cannot by defined by a boundary. The ultimate reality is unbounded and unlimited, which is to say it is infinite.

The very fact that everything is defined by a boundary implies that everything is differentiated. The boundary in space and time is what defines the distinct thing, and in the process differentiates that distinct thing from all other distinct things.

The construction of the boundary is the differentiation process. All distinct things are constructed and this construction process is a differentiation process. Even the world itself is created through a differentiation process involving the construction of a boundary that we call a cosmic horizon. Logic tells us that if everything in the world is constructed through a differentiation process, if the world itself is created through a differentiation process, then the source of everything in the world and the source of the world itself must be undifferentiated. To say that the ultimate reality is undifferentiated in some sense is to say that it is "one".

We seem to have a paradox. The ultimate reality is unbounded and infinite, but it is also undifferentiated and "one". The paradox only gets worse. Since the ultimate reality is the source of everything including the world itself, logic tells us that the ultimate reality cannot be some distinct thing that we can delineate and identify in the world. The source of all distinct things cannot itself be a distinct limited thing. To say that the ultimate reality is not some distinct limited thing is to say that it is "no-thing".

The unbounded, unlimited, undifferentiated nature of ultimate reality as the source of all distinct things, including the world itself, tells us that the ultimate reality is infinite, "one" and "no-thing". The ultimate reality can only be described as the infinite, unbounded, undifferentiated nothingness that is the source of all distinct things.

Chapter 4. The Ultimate Reality and Nature of Consciousness

The distinct things, including the world itself, are always limited and defined by a boundary in space and time. The distinct things, including the world itself, are all finite, bounded, and differentiated. The ultimate reality as the source of all the distinct things is not definable in this way, but is only describable in negative terms or in terms of what it is not: as unlimited, as unbounded, as undifferentiated, and as nothingness.

There is one last indefinable aspect of ultimate reality that is deducible from logic and reason alone. Every distinct thing in the world is perceivable but the nature of the perception of things is a mystery that science can never solve. We have no credible scientific explanation for our ability to perceive the perceivable things. There is no scientific theory that explains our ability to perceive things.

It is logically impossible that the source of our ability to perceive things can somehow emerge from the perceivable things themselves. The irrefutable expression of this logical impossibility are the Gödel incompleteness theorems. If the perceivable things are described by a consistent set of computational rules, as is the case in all scientific theories, then the ability to know about the consistency of the rules cannot itself emerge from the rules. The emergence of the ability to know about the consistency of the rules from the rules would imply a paradox of self-reference and that paradox would make the rules logically inconsistent. Logical consistency absolutely requires the ability to know about the consistency of the rules cannot itself emerge from the computational rules.

The ability to know about the consistency of the computational rules is a mystery that any science based on consistent computational rules can never explain. In exactly the same way, the ability to perceive the perceivable things cannot itself emerge from the perceivable things. What is the source of this ability to perceive the perceivable things? The only possible answer is the source of the ability to perceive the perceivable things is the very same source that is the source of the perceivable things. The ultimate reality is the source of all the distinct perceivable things and it is also the source of the ability to perceive the perceivable things.

The ability to perceive the distinct perceivable things is what we mean by the word *consciousness*. This tells us that the ultimate reality is not only the source of all the distinct perceivable things, but it is also the source of the consciousness that perceives the perceivable things. The ultimate reality is the infinite, unbounded, undifferentiated nothingness that is not only the source of all distinct things; it is also the source of the consciousness that perceives all the perceivable things.

Modern cosmology tells us that just like all the perceivable things in the world, the world itself is a distinct perceivable thing defined and limited by the boundary of a cosmic horizon. The cosmic horizon is a bounding surface of space that surrounds the observer at the central point of view. Modern physics tells us the cosmic horizon acts as a holographic screen that encodes all the fundamental quantized bits of information that define everything observable in the observer's world.

21 | *Chapter 4. The Ultimate Reality and Nature of Consciousness*

In the language of quantum theory, the holographic screen constructs a Hilbert space of observable values for all possible observations the observer can make in its world. This construction of a Hilbert space on a holographic screen is possible in a non-commutative geometry when position coordinates on the bounding surface of space are represented by non-commuting variables. In this scenario, each fundamental pixel defined on the screen encodes a fundamental quantized bit of information.

The holographic principle tells us that all perceivable things are composed of bits of information and the perception of anything is like the projection of a form of information from the screen to the central point of view of the observer. The observer's holographic screen is the boundary in space and time that defines its world; a world that by its very nature is finite, bounded and differentiated. The observer itself can only be understood as the consciousness present at the central point of view of that world.

The ultimate reality is not only the source of everything in the observer's world, it is also the source of the observer's world. Modern physics tells us the observer's world is constructed on the holographic screen that surrounds the observer at the central point of view. That is where all the bits of information are encoded. The observer's holographic screen is the boundary that delineates and defines the observer's world.

The observer's finite, bounded, differentiated world can only become constructed when a boundary arises in the midst of the infinite, unbounded, undifferentiated nothingness of ultimate reality. Even more remarkable than this conclusion is that the ultimate reality is also the source of the observer's consciousness. The observer's consciousness is present at the central point of view of its world but is only present when its world is differentiated from the undifferentiated nothingness of ultimate reality. The differentiation process is the construction of the boundary. Not only is the observer's world differentiated from the ultimate reality, the observer's consciousness is also differentiated from the ultimate reality.

The construction of this boundary and the encoding of information on the boundary requires the expenditure of energy, which is equivalent to the exertion of a force. In relativity theory, we understand the nature of forces as an accelerated frame of reference. The boundary is an event horizon that only arises in an accelerated frame of reference, which requires the expenditure of energy. The space and time that characterize the observer's world, along with all the information that defines everything in the observer's world, can only arise with the expenditure of energy that constructs the boundary.

Where does this energy come from? Like everything else in the observer's world, the ultimate reality is the source of this energy. We even have a name for this primordial energy, which we call dark energy. The construction of the cosmic horizon is due entirely to the force of dark energy. Even the flow of time is a consequence of this expenditure of energy. Without this expenditure of energy, there is no horizon, there is no bounded space, and there is no flow of time. Without this expenditure of energy, there is no construction of a boundary, there is no differentiation of a world or the consciousness that perceives that world, and there is no time-bound world. Without the construction of the boundary, the unbounded, undifferentiated nothingness is timeless and unchanging.

An odd aspect of relativity theory is the total energy of the world can add up to zero, since the negative potential energy of gravitational attraction can exactly cancel out all positive forms of energy, like dark energy, mass energy and kinetic energy. Since everything in that world is composed of energy, and all of that energy can add up to zero, everything can ultimately be nothing. Observations indicate the total energy of the universe is exactly zero, and so everything in the world ultimately adds up to nothing.

The ultimate reality is the infinite, unbounded, undifferentiated, unchanging nothingness. It is not only the source of the observer's world and the source of everything in that world, but it is also the source of the observer's consciousness that perceives all the distinct perceivable things in its world, even when that perceivable thing is the world itself.

The observer's world only appears and the observer is only present for that world when energy is expended and a boundary arises in the midst of the primordial nothingness. When energy is no longer expended, the boundary is no longer constructed, the observer's world disappears, and the observer is no longer present. When energy is no longer expended, when space is no longer bounded and time no longer flows, only the observer's underlying reality remains. That underlying reality is the source of the observer's consciousness. This underlying reality, this *ground of being*, is the infinite, unbounded, undifferentiated, unchanging, primordial nothingness that is called ultimate reality.

The ultimate reality can be described as infinite, "one-ness" and "no-thing-ness"; but what it cannot be described as is "two-ness". Only the emergent reality of an observer and its world can be described as "two-ness". This duality is a direct consequence of the fact that an observer's world contains information about discrete observable things, and these bits of information are encoded in a binary code, like numerical variables that take on the discrete values 1 or 0, or spin variables that take on the discrete values *up* or *down*.

Duality is a direct consequence of the way bits of information are encoded on a bounding surface of space. Non-commutative geometry gives a natural explanation for duality in terms of non-commuting variables. Only a boundary arising in the midst of the primordial nothingness differentiates an observer and its world from the ultimate reality. In its ultimate, unbounded, undifferentiated, primordial state, reality can only be described as non-dual.

Now let us see how we may arrive at the same conclusion about the ultimate reality with the help of physics and the wisdom of the ancients.

From the moment of the Big Bang event the universe has been expanding at an accelerated pace from the point of view of an observer at the central point of view due to the repulsive force of dark energy. The accelerated frame of reference is what gives rise to a boundary in space. The boundary in an accelerated frame of reference from the point of an observer at the central point of view is understood as the event horizon. The nature of the frame of reference defines the boundary and the boundary in turn defines the geometrical nature of the bounded space. The observer's accelerated frame of reference always implies expenditure of energy and it is only this expenditure of energy that defines the nature of the bounded space.

Inflationary cosmology hypothesizes that at the moment of the big bang event, the cosmological constant, Λ was about 1 and the size of the universe, R about a Planck length, 10^{-33} centimeter. The cosmological constant Λ has been decreasing ever since to its current value of 10^{-123} as the dark energy has been burning away and the size of the universe has inflated to its current size of about 10^{62} Planck lengths, or 15 billion light-years. The structural edifice of relativity theory is built on the principle of equivalence, whose first principle postulates that gravity is equivalent to an accelerated frame of reference, implying that there is a frame of reference, called a freely falling frame of reference, in which the force of gravity would disappear. For this reason, gravity is deemed as a fictitious (or gauge) force in that it can vanish in a freely falling frame of reference. The only way known to unify the other three fundamental forces (electromagnetism, strong and weak nuclear forces) with gravity is the Kaluza-Klein mechanism, which gives a geometrical explanation in terms of six extra compactified dimensions. This is inherent in string theory and M-theory. With such a geometrical unification, the idea of a freely falling frame of reference applies to all four fundamental forces. Thus, the four fundamental forces exist only because the universe is in an accelerated frame of reference from the point of the observer at the central point of view.

Mathematically, a freely falling frame of reference is only a coordinate transformation. For example, if the force of gravity is constant throughout space, say directed in the x-direction in a coordinate system called (x, y, z, t), the acceleration due to gravity is simply a = g directed in the x-direction. By a simple coordinate transformation $x' = x - \frac{1}{2}gt^2$, into a new coordinate system labeled (x', y, z, t), the force of gravity disappears. This new coordinate system is called a freely falling frame of reference. Once all four fundamental forces have a unified geometrical basis, even when some of the dimensions are compactified, it is always possible to find a coordinate system in which all four forces vanish. This is only a transformation of a coordinate system. We then interpret this coordinate transformation in terms of the observations that are made by an observer present at the origin or the central point of view of that coordinate system. For gravity, the observer falls freely through the 3+1 extended dimensions of space-time, while for the other three gauge forces the observer falls freely through the extra compactified dimensions. This makes perfectly good sense if the observer is present at a point in space-time, and follows a worldline through space-time.

The solution to Einstein's equations with a positive cosmological constant gives the metric for an exponentially-expanding space in which every observer at the central point of view is surrounded by a cosmic horizon. At the cosmic horizon, things appear to move away from the observer at the speed of light. Since nothing can travel faster than the speed of light, the cosmic horizon is as far out in space as the observer at the central point of view can see things in space. The cosmic horizon is a bounding surface of space that limits the observer's observations in space due to the limitation of the speed of light.

The remarkable conclusion of modern physics as it attempts to unify relativity theory with quantum theory is that the horizon acts as a holographic screen that surrounds the observer at the central point of view and encodes all the bits of information for the observer's world. This holographic scenario is how the observer's world is defined in modern physics. Amanda Gefter (2014) refers to this as the one-world-per-observer paradigm.

The nature of cosmic horizon as a bounding surface of space surrounding an observer at the central point of view has profound implications due to the nature of Hawking radiation, horizon complementarity, and the holographic principle. The inevitable conclusion of these discoveries is the one-world-per-observer paradigm. This paradigm tells us that everything observable in the world is inherently observer-dependent. Quantum theory can only be understood in a way that makes any real sense in terms of the one-world-per-observer paradigm. Each observer has its own world defined in its own frame of reference, within which a holographic screen arises. Each observer's holographic screen is a bounding surface of space that surrounds the observer at the central point of view and encodes quantized bits of information for that world, with one bit of information encoded per pixel on the screen, and so each observer has its own Hilbert space that describes all possible observations in its own world.

The idea of quantum theory is a natural extension of relativity theory. The natural definition of action is in terms of the geometrical length of a worldline, which is a path through the geometry followed by an observer. Relativity theory only allows for the path of least action. In quantum theory, all possible paths are allowed. Each possible worldline is weighted with a probability factor called the wave function that depends on the action, or the geometrical length of the worldline. The path of least action is like the shortest distance between two points in a curved space-time geometry, but quantum theory allows for all possible paths.

The natural consequence of this quantization procedure is a Hilbert space that describes all possible observable values of all observable things observed in the observer's world as the observer follows some possible worldline through the geometry. The holographic principle and the one-world-per-observer paradigm tell us that each observer has its own Hilbert space of all observable values of everything observed in the observer's world defined on its own holographic screen. A consensual reality shared by many observers is possible since their holographic screens can overlap. An observer's holographic screen is only a bounding surface of space that arises because the observer is in an accelerated frame of reference. The holographic principle tells us all information for the observer's world is encoded on a bounding surface of space that acts as a holographic screen, which only arises because the observer is in an accelerated frame of reference.

Chapter 4. The Ultimate Reality and Nature of Consciousness

In an ultimate freely falling frame of reference, all the gauge forces and the force of dark energy disappear. There is no bounding surface of space, no event horizon and no holographic screen, and all observable things in the observer's world disappear. When everything in the observer's world disappears, only the observer's underlying reality remains. Since there is nothing in that ultimate reality, we call it the void. If everything in the observer's world is observer-dependent and can disappear in an ultimate freely falling frame of reference, then what is ultimately real? What is the observer's underlying reality? The only possible answer is the source of the observer's consciousness. We call the primordial, undifferentiated source of the observer's consciousness the void. The ultimate reality is the nothingness of the void.

If the observer is a macroscopic physical body that must occupy a large amount of space, then this interpretation does not make any sense. Obviously, a macroscopic physical body cannot fall freely through a microscopic compactified dimension, but a point of consciousness can. If the observer is identified with a point of consciousness at the central point of view of a holographic screen, then the idea of a freely falling frame of reference, in the sense of a mathematical coordinate transformation, makes perfect sense. On the other hand, if the observer is identified with a macroscopic physical body, then it doesn't. The mathematics doesn't change, but the interpretation does. Since the holographic screen encodes all the information for a world, the observer present at the central point of view of the screen can enter into an ultimate state of free fall in which the effects of all forces disappear, the screen disappears, and the observer's world disappears. In the process of falling into the void, the observer has the direct experience of the void, but in reality, this is the ultimate experience of "being the void".

Physical explanations can never explain consciousness and can never explain free will, which can only arise with the focus of attention of consciousness. Biology cannot explain consciousness and free will nor can consciousness emerge from a biological body by some unexplained mechanism. Biological emergent mechanism for consciousness is not possible as the Gödel's incompleteness theorems prove that any kind of emergent mechanism is impossible. The consciousness that knows about the consistency of the rules cannot itself emerge from any mechanism obeying a consistent set of rules. Incompleteness is a consequence of the measurement of a finite amount of information. No such finite measurement can ever prove the consistency of the rules, and yet consciousness knows about the consistency of the rules. How is this knowledge possible? The answer is intuition which can never be reduced to a finite measurement of information. Where does intuition come from? It comes from the source of consciousness, which is infinite, and can only be described as the infinite nothingness of the void. No "theory of everything" can ever explain consciousness, since it cannot explain this infinite nothingness. There is a way to prove the existence of this infinite nothingness as an experiment of one. This experiment of one is called enlightenment. You can prove the existence of the infinite nothingness for yourself because you can become enlightened and have the direct experience of it. You can have the direct experience of being it.

Chapter 4. The Ultimate Reality and Nature of Consciousness

The source of the observer's consciousness is not something that can be found in the physical reality of the observer's world, but can only be found in the underlying reality that remains when everything in that physical reality disappears. That ultimate, underlying reality is the source of the observer's consciousness, but it can only be described as the void.

The mystery of the observable world is that nothing *appears* to become something (Gefter, 2014) when a boundary arises in the infinite, undifferentiated empty space. A bounding surface of space holographically constructs a Hilbert space for the observer's world which arises when the observer is in an accelerated frame of reference surrounding the observer at the central point of view. In an ultimate freely falling frame of reference, the boundary disappears, and so too does everything in the observer's world. The nothingness that remains can be called an Absence, but in reality what remains is a Presence, since it is the source of consciousness. What is seen as an Absence when one looks outwardly at the world may be seen to be a Presence when one looks within. The explanation of consciousness strongly resonates with the verse, Nasadiya Sukta in the Rig Veda (RV 10.130). The Book of Genesis calls it the void while Plato, the Source, and Shankara calls it Brahman. The Observer in Modern Physics is Atman while the source of consciousness is Brahman.

Further Reading

[1] **Gefter, Amanda**, *Trespassing on Einstein's Lawn: A Father, a Daughter, the Meaning of Nothing, and the Beginning of Everything* Random House, 2014.

[2] **Kowall, James P.**, The Physicist's Dilemma: Ultimate Reality – The Non-Physical Nature of Consciousness, Journal of Consciousness & Research, 5. 4. 2014 pp. 392 – 396.

CHAPTER 5
Who Am I

Let us see how Yoga arrives at the same conclusion as logic and modern physics in Chapter 4. Yoga means to connect and what aspires to connect is Atmanic consciousness to Brahmanic consciousness. At the moment of the Big Bang event the size of the universe was the Planck length (10^{-33} cm in diameter) and everything in the universe was connected to everything else and it would remain so indefinitely. Scientific evidence in support of this hypothesis is presented later in the book. This evidence suggests that our individual consciousness (Atmanic consciousness) is a microcosm of the cosmic consciousness (Brahmanic consciousness). The feeling of disconnection of our individual consciousness from the cosmic consciousness is the leading cause for all sorts of problems in our lives. How to go about strengthening this link is what this book all about. We need to rationally and experientially convince our hearts and minds that our higher self is a microcosm of the cosmic consciousness. Then progress will be easier. It is in this context, the age old inquiry, *'Who Am I* assumes significance. The difficulty is that individual consciousness and cosmic consciousness cannot be accessed with scientific theories or equations nor can they be directly measured. We can get tantalizing close to answering the question but we can never answer it satisfactorily with a probability of 1.0.

This chapter presents two perspectives on this all important query. The first is an English-language adaptation of a few discourses of self-realized yogi Baba Shivanand Ji on Z TV in which he explains how we could improve all aspects of our lives even with a rudimentary understanding of who we are, and the second is how an American theoretical physicist turned medical doctor, inspired by the work of Rig Veda, Geeta, Genesis, Plato, Shankara, and Nisargadatta responds to the same question. As you delve into this chapter, remember Nikola Tesla's remark on Page VI, '*If you want to understand the universe, think of energy, frequency, and vibration*'. Also remember Nisargadatta's remark on the same page, *What you seek is so near you that there is no space for a way*. Add emotions to the list and ponder which laws of physics can explain the effect of emotions on anything.

5.1 Adaptation of Baba Shivanand Ji's Discourses, 'I Am That, I Am' (June – July 2014 on Z TV)

If you were asked a question, 'Are you the body or is the body yours?' We are sure you would say, 'The body is mine'. If you were asked, 'Are you the mind or is the mind yours?' you would answer, 'The mind is mine'. Naturally the question arises, if you are different from my body, different from my mind, who are you?

Upanishad says, '*Man hi karta, manhi bhogta*, meaning the mind creates and the mind suffers. The mind creates sorrow and then cries of its own creation. The mind creates some difficulty, gets entrapped in it, and suffers from what it has created. Now, if you come to realize that the mind is yours, shouldn't you be able to control your mind or not? You could say, *'Mind, you are not the Karta (Master), I am; you cannot just do whatever you want, you will have to do what I tell you to do'*. Similarly, since you are the owner of the body, you could command, *'Body, you will have to obey my command, not do whatever you want; that is unacceptable'*.

Being the master of your body, senses, and the mind, you are the owner of an IT super technology system, much more powerful than any supercomputer and therefore, shouldn't you have an intimate understanding of your body and the mind? Of course, you should. Let us take an analogy. When you buy a computer system with a super-fast central processing unit, lots of internal memory & RAM, peripheral accessories, and a great operating system, what happens? The computer is delivered to your home or office. A computer technician comes in, takes it out of the box, assembles it, plugs it into the electrical socket, boots it up, and makes sure everything is operating properly. Then, someone trains you in the use of your system so you can begin to operate it. So, the steps are delivery, installation, learning or training, and operation, not the surgical type.

Let us see what happens with us human beings. The expectant mother goes to the hospital and delivers a baby. The *model* is a boy or a girl, great. So the delivery is made but where is the installation? Who provided the training, and where is the operation? Everyone is delivered but we never get installed, learn who we are, acquire the knowledge of ourselves. Those processes are missing. In ancient times, Guru Diksha (teachings by a guru) used to be important. In childhood, the young would be sent to an ashram to get installed. There, pupils would not only study subjects of contemporary importance, but also gain the knowledge of one's inner capabilities, and after learning all this, they would return home ready to go into operation.

Now look at the irony of it. You are the owner of an ultrafast CPU, trillions of GB of memory, much more powerful than any computer, equipped with natural intelligence not its artificial counterpart, sophisticated algorithms with a capacity to solve highly complex problems such as the origin of matter, beginning of the universe, how space-time warps around massive gravitational objects producing the effect of bending of light, but the system just remains in the box, never even opened. Three percent of our DNA is active, the rest is junk DNA; four percent of the mind is aware but ninety-six percent is not. We are delivered in a box and go back in a box. So, what does the Maker do? Send us back again and again giving opportunity after opportunity until we go through the entire process and learn who we really are. Then, there is no further need to send us back.

Although we may not know who we really are at this stage, you can be sure your body and your mind obey our commands only. Only that these commands are issued in ignorance (in Sanskrit, *Agyanatavash*). You tell your mind to imbibe negative emotions (anger, hostility, hatred, jealousy, resentment, despair, etc.), and the mind obeys. And if your life is filled with negative emotions, your physician can convince you this will have a catastrophic effect on our health and wellbeing. Elizabeth Blackburn, 2009 Nobel Prize recipient in physiology and medicine recently published a study on the aging effects of stress in the proceedings of the national Academy of Sciences (PNAS) and Nature.

So, how do we progress in our quest to know who we really are? Here is how Baba Ji explains it. The source of this wisdom is both ancient and impeccable but we will take it as a hypothesis requiring substantiation. We begin with the realization that we don't have just one body; we have five. The first is the physical body that we commonly recognize as the body and the remaining four are energy bodies or sheaths. The five bodies are: (1) Annamaya Kosha (Sharir, food sheath), (2) Pranamaya Kosha (Pranic energy sheath), (3) Manomaya Kosha (Mind sheath), (4) Dnyanamaya Kosha (Knowledge Sheath of Psychic Impressions Sheath), and (5) Anandamaya Kosha (Blissful Sheath). A schematic of the five bodies is depicted in Figure 5.1. Each energy

Figure 5.1 Schematic of the Five Bodies

sheath controls the lower sheath. Thus, Dnyanamaya Kosha controls the Manomaya Kosha which in turn controls the Pranamaya Kosha which controls the Annamaya Kosha. Each is more powerful than the one it controls. In the Dnyanamaya Kosha are stored psychic impressions and unresolved issues from the past.

Physicists tell us that some five percent of the observable universe is matter (planets, galaxies, stars, etc.), twenty-seven percent is dark matter (e. g., black holes), and sixty-eight percent is dark energy. So, there is abundant energy in the universe. Birds use this energy to make nonstop transcontinental flights. And yogis use it in meditation allowing them to go without food or drink for weeks with no loss of weight.

We too have access to this abundant reservoir of cosmic energy and our energy bodies are constantly trying to access it. The problem is that the negative psychic impressions and unresolved issues in our Dnyanamaya Kosha block it from freely flowing through our energy sheaths. If the energy channels weren't blocked, we will reach the Anandamaya Kosha, the ever blissful sheath and when we do, we will experience our higher self, *Aham Brahmasmi*, I am the creator. It is that state where our Atmanic consciousness is connected to Brahmanic consciousness. The quest to experientially know *Who Am I* boils down to being able to release the negative psychic impressions and unresolved issues in the Dnyanamaya Kosha and through the process of meditation this can be achieved.

There is scope for measurement in several places during the practices of Baba Ji for validation purposes. As you delve into this book, more and more details will be revealed.

5.2 Modern Physics Perspective

A discussion of "Who am I" needs to distinguish Brahmanic consciousness from Atmanic consciousness. Atmanic consciousness only refers to an observer and its world. In the sense of Plato's Allegory of the Cave, if all the perceivable images of that world are displayed on a holographic screen that surrounds the observer at the central point of view, then the I-Am/consciousness is only the central perceiving point.

This is how Nisargadatta describes the observer, which he calls the witness: Only the onlooker is real, call him Self or Atman. That which makes you think that *you are a human is not human*. It is a dimensionless point of consciousness, a conscious nothing. All you can say about yourself is 'I am'. You are the source of reality - a dimensionless center of perception that imparts reality to whatever it perceives - a pure witness that watches what is going on and yet remains unaffected. It is only imagination and self-identification with the imagined that encloses and converts the inner watcher into a person. Whatever happens, I remain. At the root of my being is pure awareness, a speck of intense light. This speck, by its nature, radiates and creates pictures in space and events in time, effortlessly and spontaneously.

Delve deeply into the sense of 'I am' and you will discover that the perceiving center is universal. All that happens in the universe happens to you, the silent witness. There can be no universe without the witness, no witness without the universe.

First we must know ourselves as witnesses only, dimensionless and timeless centers of observation, and then realize that there is immense ocean of pure awareness, which is both mind and matter and beyond both. Awareness is beyond all. Awareness is primordial; it is the original state.

Awareness is undivided - aware of itself. Awareness comes as if from a higher dimension.

The witness that stands aloof is the watchtower of the real- the point at which awareness, inherent in the unmanifested, contacts the manifested. I see as you see, hear as you hear. All this I perceive quite clearly, but I am not in it. I feel myself as floating over it, aloof and detached. There is also the awareness of it all and a sense of immense distance as if the body and the mind and all that happens to them were somewhere far out on the horizon.

I am like a cinema screen-clear and empty. The pictures pass over it and disappear, leaving it as clear and empty as before. In no way is the screen affected by the pictures, nor are the pictures affected by the screen. The screen intercepts and reflects the pictures. These are lumps of destiny, but not my destiny; the destinies of the people on the screen.

The character will become a person when he begins to shape his life instead of accepting it as it comes - identifying himself with it. To myself I am neither perceivable nor conceivable; there is nothing I can point out and say "this I am". I see only consciousness, and know everything to be but consciousness, as you know the pictures on the cinema screen to be but light. It is enough to shift attention from the screen onto oneself to break the spell. You look at it from the outside as you look at a play on the stage or a picture on the screen. To know the picture as the play of light on the screen gives freedom from the idea that the picture is real. The totality of all mental projections is the Great Illusion.

When I look beyond the mind I see the witness. Beyond the witness is infinite emptiness and silence.

Reality is essentially alone. To know that nothing is, is true knowledge. For the path of return naughting oneself is necessary. My stand I take where nothing is. To the mind it is all darkness and silence. It is deep and dark, mystery beyond mystery. It is while all else merely happens. It is like a bottomless well, whatever falls into it disappears.

In pure being, consciousness arises; in consciousness the world appears and disappears. Consciousness is on contact, a reflection against a surface, a state of duality. The center is a point of void and the witness a point of pure awareness; they know themselves to be as nothing. Wisdom says "I am nothing". By itself nothing has existence. Your true home is in nothingness. Nothing lasts. The void remains. You remain as pure being.

When Nisargadatta refers to "the void, pure being, the ocean of pure awareness, nothingness, or the unmanifested", he refers to the Brahmanic consciousness. Atmanic consciousness must be differentiated from Brahmanic consciousness. Brahmanic consciousness is the undifferentiated source of differentiated Atmanic consciousness. Brahmanic consciousness is the underlying reality of Atmanic consciousness. Since Atmanic consciousness is the nature of individual being, the I-Am/Consciousness, Brahmanic consciousness is the ground of being.

The Brahmanic consciousness is the ultimate state of being. It is the primordial state of being that remains when differentiated Atmanic consciousness dissolves back into the primordial, unbounded, undifferentiated Brahmanic consciousness. It is an unchanging, timeless state that has no boundary and has no information. This ultimate state of being is a state of unknowing. There is no information in it, and there is nothing to know.

Who knows what? Only the Atmanic consciousness can know about the world it perceives, a world composed of information. In the ultimate Brahmanic state of being, there is no individual consciousness to know anything, one knows nothing, and "I am not". In this ultimate state of being, the primordial nothingness knows itself as it really is, as infinite, as undivided, as one, as nothingness.

In a strange way, one purpose of creation is to allow us to ask questions and look for answers. The nature of an emergent world is you can ask questions, look for answers, and find answers, but the answers you find only apply to that emergent world. This is a kind of Catch-22. The answers do not apply to the true nature of what you are, because what you are is not really a part of this emergent world any more than a dreamer is a part of the dream it dreams into brief existence. To find answers about your true nature, you have to look outside the emergent world.

Energy must be expended to ask questions and look for answers. In the sense of the holographic principle, energy must be expended to construct a holographic screen that encodes bits of information. The very act of asking questions, looking for answers and finding the answers, constructs a holographic screen, encodes bits of information on the screen, and expends energy.

The only way this holographic screen can be deconstructed, the only way the expenditure of energy can come to an end, is if questions are no longer asked and answers are no longer looked for and found. The ultimate state of being, the primordial state of being that remains when individual Atmanic consciousness dissolves back into the primordial undifferentiated Brahmanic consciousness, is a state that has no boundary, no holographic screen, no information, and expends no energy. In this ultimate state of being, no questions are asked and no answers are found. This ultimate state of being is a state of unknowing; a state where "I am not" and one knows nothing.

References

[1] Avdhoot Baba Shivanand Ji, www.shivyog.com
[2] Blackburn, E. H. and Epel, E. S., Too Toxic to Ignore, Nature, 490, 11 October 2012. P. 169.
[3] Epel, Elissa S., et al., Accelerated Telomere Shortening in Response to Life Stress, PNAS, 101, 49, December 7, 2004.
[4] Nisargadatta Maharaj, I am That, Acorn Press, Durham Press, NC 2012 (Available on Amazon.com).

CHAPTER 6
The Two Domains of Excellence

To begin, think of the two domains of excellence as depicted in Figure 6.1: *The domain of the Unmanifest* (Brahmanic consciousness or Cosmic Consciousness) and the *domain of the manifest* (Atmanic consciousness) accessible with the five senses. All data, information, and facts from the Big Bang to the present are deemed to be in the domain of the Unmanifest while the domain of the manifest contains all there is in the manifest world in the form of a finitely infinite chain of causes and effects. The two are separated by a boundary that represents Atmanic consciousness, enlightenment (*Self Real I Zation*), the upper limit of human consciousness.

6.1 Domain of the Manifest

All there is in the domain of the manifest is in the form of causes and effects and therefore anyone of them may be selected for scrutiny if it is important for personal or business reasons and taken to be an effect, an outcome. The goal then is to insure that this outcome is in the best possible state for the best possible performance. This is made possible by six sigma co-created by Dr. Mikel Harry at Motorola in the late

46 | *Chapter 6. The Two Domains of Excellence*

seventies. The founding principles of six sigma are four natural laws:

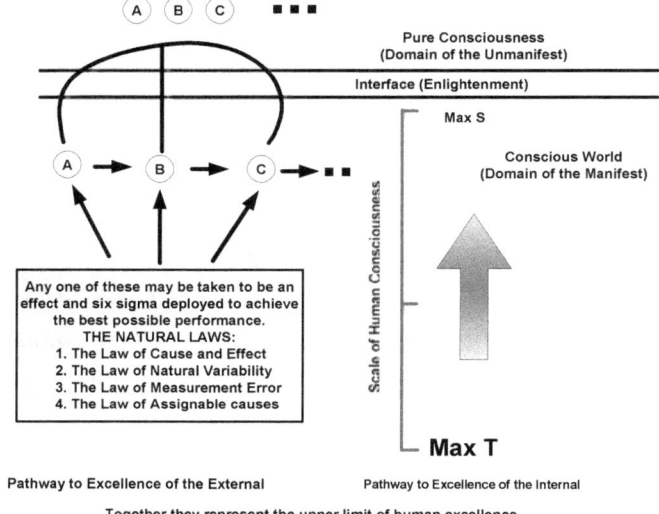

Figure 6.1 The Two Domains of Excellence

1. The Law of Cause and Effect: The first natural law states: *For every effect, there must necessarily be a cause or causes.* The effect is the outcome whose performance is sought to be improved. Although this law does not identify what the causes are, it is nonetheless a source of comfort for anyone aspiring to improve the performance of the outcome knowing that there are *causes* influencing the outcome. If these causes could be found, and they are found with six sigma, they would be worked on to improve the performance. Fundamentally, there are four types of causes and their description necessitates access to three other laws of nature.

2. The Law of Natural Variation: The second natural law, adapted from the work of German scientist Frederick Gauss, stipulates the first of these types of causes. It states, *All processes and transactions exhibit a certain amount of inherent variation no matter how well they are designed.* This natural variability occurs due to a host of unknown and uncontrollable causes called common causes. Perfection therefore (zero defects ad infinitum) is not in the plan of nature. However, adherence to the principles of six sigma will ensure that the defect levels are as small as this natural law permits them to be. In the context of the human state, the common causes are those we inherit from our ancestors plus those we generate by our own actions.

3. The Law of Discoverable Causes (USA and Japan, 20th Century AD): The third natural law, adapted from the work of several American and Japanese quality control professionals states, *The inherent variation in the outcomes of work processes due to uncontrollable/unknown causes is worsened by causes that are discoverable. Tracing and then eliminating them or setting them at the correct values as appropriate returns the outcome to its natural state.*

4. The Law of Variation Due to Measurement Error: Measurement errors further increase the variation in the outcomes of work processes and therefore defects. To achieve the desired improvement, measurement errors must constitute an acceptably small fraction of the total variation in the outcome.

Figure 6.2 graphically illustrates these ideas. The vertical line labeled Target is where the outcome should be. Figure

48 | *Chapter 6. The Two Domains of Excellence*

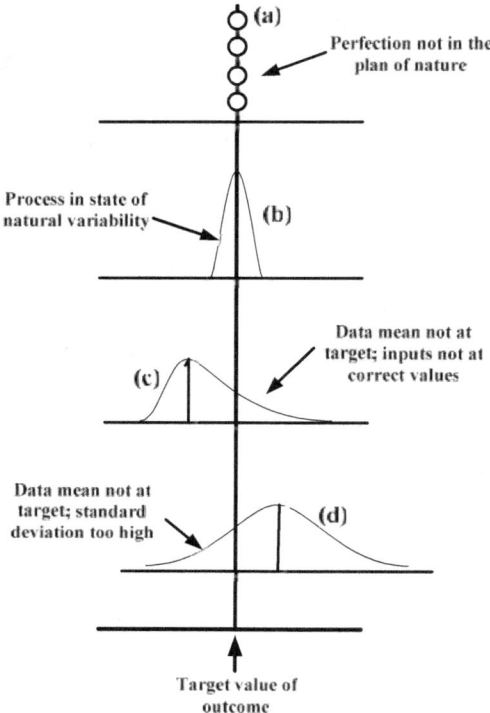

Figure 6.2 Returning the Outcome to Natural Variability

6.2(a) depicts an impossible situation where all the data points are on the target. As shown in Figure 6.2(b) there will be a certain amount of inherent variability in every process or transaction outcome consistent with the common causes as per the second natural law. This inherent variability is worsened by discoverable causes which include measurement errors. For example, the distribution may become skewed, the mean may veer off target, and the standard deviation may increase – see Figures 6.2(c) and (d) as per the third and fourth natural laws. The goal of six sigma is to return the outcome to its natural state, Figure 6.2(b).

Armed with these natural laws, it is possible to write down the five-phase eleven-step six sigma procedure: (1) Define the problem, (2) Identify outcome(s), response variable(s), (3) State project goal, (4) Prepare process map, (5) Validate measurement systems, (6) Collect data on response variable(s), (7) Compute starting defect levels, (8) Design experiments/collect data on the discoverable causes of variability together with the response variable(s), (9) Analyze data so collected and determine major impact factors, (10) Determine optimal values of major impact factors and run confirmatory runs to validate the benefits, and (11) Monitor outcomes and major impact factors so that problems once fixed stay fixed and the benefits are sustained. The complete knowhow of six sigma may be found in Harry (1995) and in the text by Deshpande (2013). There are a large number of books and references on six sigma available in the marketplace.

6.2 Atmanic Consciousness and the S, R, T Level of Consciousness

At the individual level, there are many ways to define consciousness. One is to categorize it as wakeful state, (Jagrat Avastha) dream state (Swapna Avastha), sleep state (Supta Avastha), and Blissful State (Turya Avastha). Turya Avastha is the state a yogi aspires to be in, ever connected to the Brahmanic consciousness. Another is the S, R, T level of consciousness (LOC) which is useful in the context of the aim of this book.

Every human being is deemed to have three components of the mindset that defines what he or she is. In the form of an acronym the components are denoted as S, R, and T and defined as follows:

- **S**: Truthfulness, honesty, steadfastness, equanimity;
- **R**: Attachment, bravery, ego, ambition, greed, desire to live;
- **T**: Lying, cheating, causing injury in words or deeds, sleep.

In this scheme, a minimum amount of S, R, T required is for life. An S, R, T scale of consciousness is depicted in Figure 6.3 (a). An individual at the top of the scale with S_{max}, R_{min},

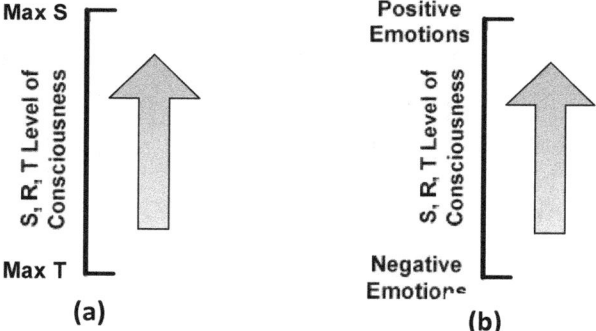

Figure 6.3. Two Equivalent Interpretations of Consciousness

T_{min} is the best a human being can be while an individual at the bottom of the sale with S_{min}, R_{min}, T_{max} is the worst a person can be. The rest of us are somewhere in between. The quest for internal excellence means to rise on this scale of consciousness. Now, a little reflection will reveal that the S component naturally and strongly correlates with positive emotions (unconditional love, empathy. kindness, compassion) while high R, and T components correlate with negative emotions (hatred, anger, guilt, hostility, jealousy, depression, resentment, despair, fear, etc.). This interpretation is depicted in Figure 6.3(b). It is possible to consciously break this correlation. For example, it is possible to cultivate a high S component but have little or no compassion. As has been pointed out again and again since ancient times, Dharma (Righteousness, high S) in the absence of Karuna (Compassion) is no virtue at all. Individuals at the top of the scale are endowed with abundant positive emotions. They will never do anything to hurt anyone or anything in words or deed. They are ever in Turya Avastha connected to Brahmanic consciousness.

In the chapters that follow we present a path forward for progress. First, the outcome measures of internal excellence which can be reliably measured are identified. Then we discuss how we might go about measuring the level of internal excellence or equivalently the S, R, T level of consciousness. Rising on the scale of consciousness is essentially an individual pursuit and so we need to know if there is something within us with which we may make progress. Several experiments of western scientists are presented to convince the reader that within each of us there in fact is something with which we may raise our level of consciousness. This is followed by a discussion of the processes for raising the level of consciousness. In the context of this discussion it becomes possible to discuss why we get ill and how we could get better. These same reasons also lead to suboptimal performance in all walks of life including business performance, discord and violence, etc.

An explanation of the importance of six sigma is presented next. Six sigma is not just a quality initiative but a fundamental systemic methodology for problem solving in the domain of the manifest. Therefore, it is the scientific framework for excellence of all external activities. The quest to raise the level of consciousness is the framework for the excellence of the internal. To be one's best means we must excel in both frameworks of excellence. What may not be obvious is that the two frameworks are intimately linked. One without the other is inadequate. In an ensuing chapter the importance of internal excellence in six sigma programs is discussed and evidence presented to substantiate the claim. Furthermore, it will become clear that the pursuit of internal excellence is itself a comprehensive six sigma problem.

The final set of chapters are intended to show the power of collective consciousness and how to harness it to promote societal and global peace. The scientific framework for internal excellence explains at the fundamental level why feelings of racial, caste-based, or religious superiority has no basis in fact. This understanding should promote interfaith understanding and racial harmony.

CHAPTER 7
How to Measure Consciousness

The first step in a project on raising the level of consciousness is to devise a scale for S, R, T levels of consciousness. Such a scale has been derived on the basis of the three natural laws articulated in Chapter 3 which were used to develop the theory of rise and decline of cultures. Human actions are determined by three components of the mindset: (i) The S component – truthfulness, honesty, equanimity, steadfastness, non-covetousness. (ii) The R component - Attachment, bravery, ambition, ego, greed, desire to live, (iii) The T component - Lying cheating, causing injury in words or deed, lethargy, excessive sleep. The 6 ½ billion inhabitants of Earth have a unique combination of these three components that determines who they are. The actions of an individual with a high S component are generally expected to be good while those of an individual with a high T component are generally expected to be bad. The definition of the three components tells us that a minimum amount of each is required to make life. This has been true for thousands of years and it will be true for thousands of years in the future, unless nature decides to change its own natural laws.

7.1 Scale of Consciousness

The *S, R, T* components permit us to propose a Scale of human consciousness. The numerical scales shown in Figure 7.1(a) for the *S, R, T* components are arbitrary but chosen to lead to a maximum value of 1000 for the Scale of Consciousness shown in Figure 7.1(b).

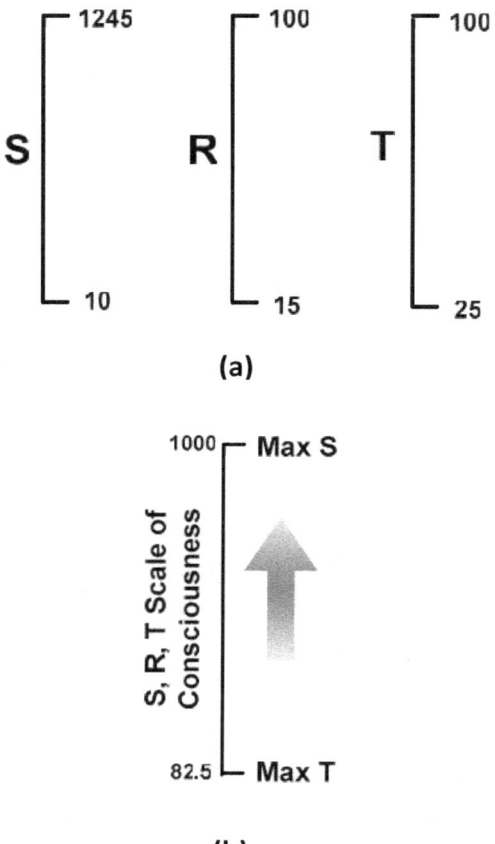

Figure 7.1. Scale of S, R, T Consciousness

Chapter 7. How to Measure Consciousness

To derive the high and low limits for the Scale of Human Consciousness from the S, R, T components, it is assumed that the three components are fractions summing to 1 and that the minimum fraction of each component required for life is 0.1. Therefore, the maximum fraction of any one of these components is 0.8. These assumptions lead to the Scale of Consciousness shown in Figure 7.1(b). The highest value for the Scale of Consciousness is derived from the formula:

$$LoC_{Max} = f_{1,Max}S_{Max} + f_{2,Min}R_{Min} + f_{3,Min}T_{Min}$$
$$= (0.8)(1245) + (0.1)(15) + (0.1)(25) \quad (7.1a)$$
$$= 1000$$

And the minimum value is computed from the formula:

$$LoC_{Min} = f_{1,Min}S_{Min} + f_{2,Min}R_{Min} + f_{3,Max}T_{Max}$$
$$= (0.1)(10) + (0.1)(15) + (0.8)(100) \quad (7.1b)$$
$$= 82.5$$

Thus, in the scheme depicted, each of us would have a level of consciousness somewhere in the range of 82.5 to 1000. The domain of Atmanic consciousness lies just beyond the top end of this Scale of Consciousness. The scale of consciousness is likely nonlinear accommodating chaotic orbits and strange attracters thus making it possible for an individual to traverse the entire distance on the scale of consciousness in very short order or to make it nearly impossible for some to make progress. Historical evidence supports this point of view.

7.2 How to Measure the Level of Consciousness

With a scale of consciousness at hand, the next task is to find a way to measure it. Ancient references to the unmanifest world and Akashik Records notwithstanding no one had found a way to measure the level of consciousness until recently. Dr. David R. Hawkins (MD, Medical College of Wisconsin 1953; Established as Marquette University School of Medicine), appears to have succeeded in that effort with the help of Kinesiology and muscle testing pioneered by Dr. John Diamond, MD. He asserts that the human nervous system is capable of downloading the information, data, facts, etc., from the unmanifest to the manifest domain with muscle testing, a test procedure used by the International College of Applied Kinesiology. This method requires two persons, a tester and a subject. The tester places two fingers of say his/her left hand on the wrist of the extended right hand of the subject so that it is at a right angle to the subject's body. The tester rests his/her right hand on the left shoulder of the subject for balance. Then, the tester makes a declarative statement having correct and incorrect responses and tells the subject to resist as he quickly applies downward pressure on the wrist. Dr. Hawkins found that the subject resisted the downward force and the deltoid muscle remained strong if the declarative statement was correct but would go weak if the declarative statement was false. Dr. Hawkins and his research group recapitulated Thomas Edison's search of 1,600 materials to arrive at Tungsten as the material for the filament of an incandescent bulb in less than ten minutes. He subjected the results of over four thousand calibrations to χ^2 tests of hypothesis testing producing favorable p-values.

Monte et al., healthcare professionals affiliated with Philadelphia-area medical schools, conducted a muscle-test investigation with 87 college students in a psychology class and reported that the correct and incorrect responses to declarative statements could be distinguished from the plots of applied force versus time (Monte, et al., 1999). They used a computer-assisted dynamometer in the investigation to eliminate human bias. Here too, the p-values were favorable. The results of their investigation are depicted in Figure 7.2. However, in this investigation, the subjects knew what the correct responses were (e. g., my name is ... OR I am a US citizen). When downloading from the domain of the unmanifest to the domain of the manifest the subjects would not know what the correct response is. It is remarkable that Dr. Hawkins and his researchers obtained correct responses even under these circumstances 97% of the time.

It is essential to investigate the measurement issue further. Six sigma principles tell us that there are five attributes of a measurement device, whether or not it is a physical device: (1) Accuracy, (2) Stability, (3) Linearity, (4) Repeatability, and (5) Reproducibility. Proceeding in a project without measurement validation can lead to catastrophic results. This is because the variability in an outcome should arise from major impact factors (so that we could discover and fix them) and not from errors in the measurement systems. In the present context, what requires validation is this: *"Can muscle testing with a dynamometer-based measurement system provide correct responses within a prescribed error tolerance (say ± 3%) even when the subjects have no knowledge of the topic"?*

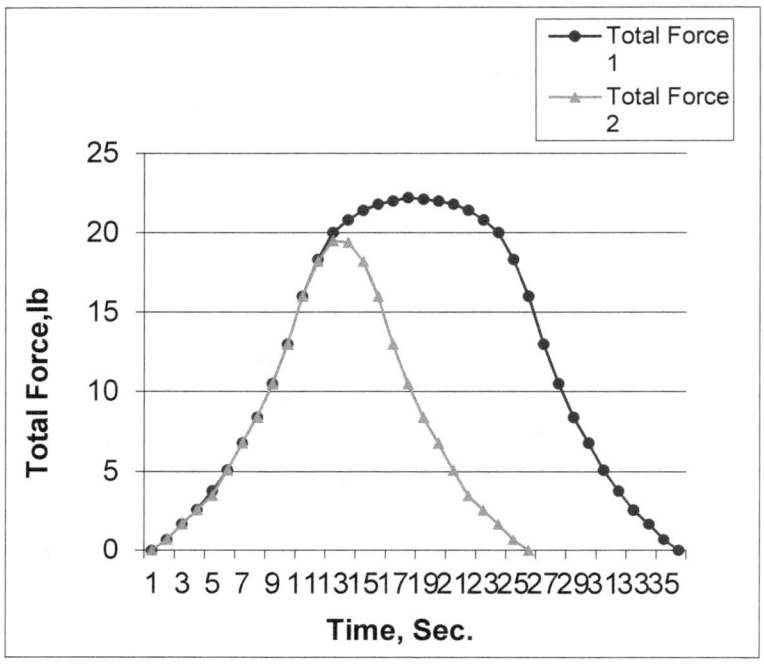

Figure 7.2. Applied Force vs. Congruent & Incongruent Responses (Included with Permission from Daniel A. Monti, MD)

Equally important, Dr. Hawkins also developed what he referred to as a Map of Human Consciousness. The resulting logarithmic scale is shown in Table 7.1. He identified numerous attributes corresponding to different levels of Consciousness. Using muscle testing he calibrated the level of consciousness of numerous individuals and works. For example, he calibrated Jesus, Sri Krishna, Buddha whom he called Avatars, (Sanskrit for Incarnation) at 1,000; Mahatma Gandhi, Mother Theresa, and the US Constitution at 700; eminent scientists like Newton and Einstein at 499, and the likes of Hitler well below 250.

Figure 7.1 and Table 7.1 may be seen to be strikingly similar. Although independently developed, the first author had pegged the three incarnations at the top of the scale of consciousness. Others listed above would occupy a position between the high and low limits.

Table 7.1. Hawkins' Map of Consciousness

Level	Score (Log$_{10}$)
Enlightenment	1,000
Joy	540
Love	500
Reason	400
Acceptance	350
Willing	310
Neutral	250
Courage	200
Pride	175
Anger	150
Desire	125
Fear	100
Guilt	30
Shame	20

7.3 The Brahma Uncertainty Principle

Quantum mechanics tells that two things about a quantum phenomenon cannot be precisely known simultaneously, for example position and momentum. If one is accurately measured the other will be in error. This is the Heisenberg Uncertainty Principle. Each of the 6 ½ billion of us has a varying level of consciousness. Therefore, if experiments which involve human consciousness are conducted the results cannot be the same. This is a huge problem for science for it expects the results of every experiment to be repeatable and reproducible regardless of who conducts the experiment, how many times, and where. The readers of the book need to be acutely aware of this uncertainty. Let us take an example.

Japanese scientist the Late Dr. Masaru Emoto, reports that beautiful and intricate water crystals result when prayer is spoken over it. According to Dr. Emoto, an ice crystal of distilled water exhibits a basic hexagonal structure with no intricate branching. Emoto claims that positive changes to water crystals can be achieved through prayer, music or by attaching written words to a water container (http://en.wikipedia.org/wiki/Masaru_Emoto). Figure 7.3 is a photograph of the water crystal before and after prayer taken from the internet.

In the context of the discussion in this section, if numerous testers were to conduct this experiment, not all will succeed. There are numerous other examples. In a number of

61 | *Chapter 7. How to Measure Consciousness*

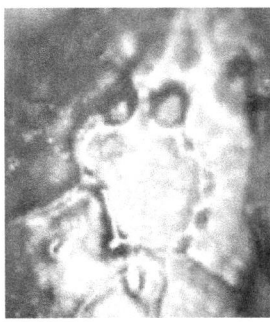
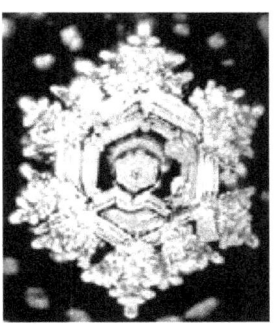

(a) Before Prayer   **(b) After Prayer**

Figure 7.3 Water Crystals Before and After Prayer

meditation programs, some 20% to 30% of the participants were seen to experience unusual results such as an expression of sheer joy, a peaceful and blissful state, spontaneous levitation, etc., but not everyone. Furthermore, participants may or may not experience this state every time. We hypothesize that in all of these examples the missing major impact factor responsible for the inability to reproduce the results every time in every case is the level of consciousness of the experimenter and/or the subject if any. Since in ancient Eastern thought, the name of Brahma is associated with pure consciousness, we have coined the name *The Brahma Uncertainty Principle* for this principle. We state the principle as follows:

Notwithstanding experimental error, the inability to reproduce a previously validated observation means that the level of consciousness of the experimenter or the subject is inadequate.

Consciousness pervades in everything that exists and therefore it is logical to surmise that the Brahma Uncertainty Principle is operational at all levels of existence including the physical and nonphysical. In the following paragraphs we present the rationale for why we believe this principle is true and present some experiments to back up our claim.

7.4 Simpler Way to Measure LOC

Here, we present a simpler method for measuring the level of consciousness. The measurement device is a crystal pendulum hung with a chain and a glass bead attached at the other end (see Figure 7.4). These pendulums are available commercially for a low price for anyone who desires to conduct these experiments. Some demonstration experiments with the pendulum may be found on YouTube (Deshpande Experiments).

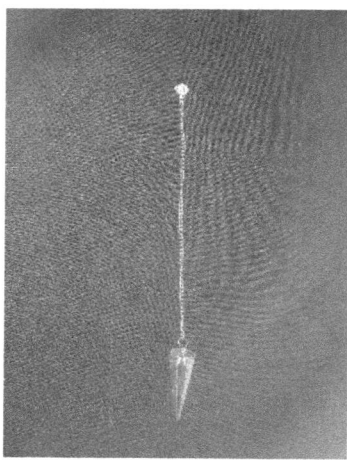

Figure 7.4. Crystal Pendulum

For the purposes of this work, the crystal pendulum may be used in one of two ways:

1. **To measure the level of consciousness of an individual**: Hold the pendulum by the bead in the two fingers of your hand and once the pendulum begins to oscillate in a back-and-forth manner, make the declarative statement, "*On a scale of 100 to 1,000, the level of consciousness of xxxx*" *is*, and then start counting from 100 upwards in increments of say 50. At the correct level of consciousness, the pendulum should start rotating.

2. **To discern truth from falsehood**. To discern truth from falsehood, hold the pendulum by the two fingers of your hand and make a declarative statement which has a true or false answer. The experimenter is not expected to know what the correct answer is. For false declarative statements, the pendulum is expected to move in a pendulum-like manner and rotate clockwise for correct responses. An interesting property of the pendulum device is also revealed when used with life-supporting and life-detrimental foods and drinks. When held a couple of inches over foods and drinks, the pendulum is expected to rotate clockwise looking down for positive pranic foods, counterclockwise for negative pranic foods, and back-and-forth for neutral foods. The latter is a small variation of the use of the measurement device for discerning truth from falsehood.

7.5 Assessing the Strength of the Principle

To ascertain the validity of the Brahma uncertainty principle we tested the pendulum device with a number of individuals with varying levels of consciousness. Each level of consciousness has an understanding of reality that is valid only at that level of perception and so we concede it is a bit presumptuous on our part to assert that we know who is at what level of consciousness. However, any experimenter would face the same dilemma.

The experiments involve two identical bottles filled to the same level, one with drinking water and the other with alcohol. We then presented the two bottles one at a time and asked the subject to hold the pendulum a couple of inches over the open bottle. The subject must not know what the content of the specific bottle presented is although a colorless liquid in both bottles is visible. Here, the pendulum has two possible motions: clockwise and counterclockwise. Over water, the pendulum is expected to rotate clockwise looking down and counterclockwise over alcohol. Many individuals are able to produce the correct motion of the pendulum if they are aware which bottle has what. The level of consciousness comes into play when the tester does not know the content of the bottle. With each subject the experiment is repeated five times giving us % correct responses.

We have observed that with some individuals, the pendulum does not produce any motion while with some others correct answers are obtained some of the time. Of specific interest are yogis, saints, and healers. We selected an enlightened

Indian yogi and an American healer, the latter with a Ph. D. in psychology, with whom we have had the good fortune to interact. Both of them produced one hundred percent correct answers. We are confident that if this experiment were to be repeated with enlightened ones, one hundred percent accuracy will be seen. We are aware that for hypothesis testing the experiments would be configured somewhat differently but it is equally true that the probability of getting all five correct answers in a row by chance is small. Our experience and these experiments have led to the plot of *Level of Consciousness* vs. *% Correct Answers* shown in Figure 7.5. It basically envisions individuals into three categories; ones who calibrate low, those who are in the middle with rising level of consciousness, and a third with a high level of consciousness. The plot is believed to be accurate in the qualitative sense. We encourage readers to investigate this phenomenon further. Our perception is that there is a large spread at low levels of consciousness which shrinks at increasing levels of consciousness as depicted in Figure 7.5.

It did not come as a surprise to us to find that the two referenced individuals who calibrated high were endowed with abundant positive emotions (compassion, love, kindness, empathy) while the individuals who calibrated low appeared to have a high a sense of ego, etc. The ability to discern truth from falsehood has a myriad of powerful applications with enormous material benefits. We were also not surprised to find that the specific individuals who calibrated high revealed little interest in materially

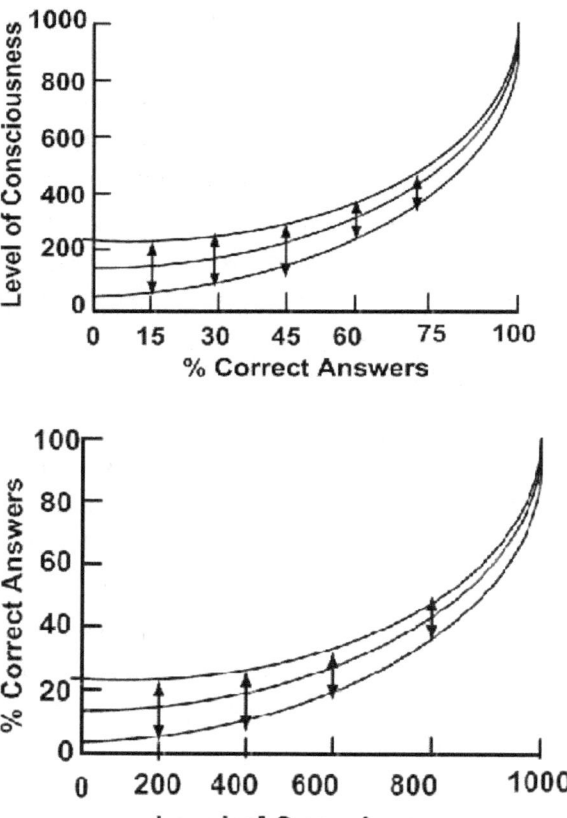

Figure 7.5. LOC vs. % Correct Answers

benefiting from their prowess. Some readers may take the concepts in this paper to be mystical. We suggest that mysticism is science not yet understood but mysticism and superstition are close cousins and therefore all observations must be validated with six sigma principles.

7.6 Underlying Principle

Neurologists tell us that our brain has motor command neurons that constantly fire. This causes a twitch ever so slight in the two fingers that hold the pendulum. The energy required for the pendulum to produce motion is really small, $\frac{1}{2} i\omega^2$ and therefore the twitch is sufficient for pendulum-like back-and-forth motion. With deliberate intention, it is possible to produce clockwise or counterclockwise motion. Now, the hypothesis is that our higher self (Atmanic consciousness) is perfectly capable of discerning truth from falsehood provided our mind does not interfere in the process. People of high level of consciousness are therefore able to discern truth from falsehood. Another way of saying this is that the domain of the unmanifest (Cosmic consciousness) has imprinted in it all data, information, facts and as long as the mind does not interfere, the same can be downloaded to the domain of the manifest with the help of the pendulum.

Yogis may have used these ideas in ancient times with the help of Rudraksha, a neckless with 108 beads which are the seeds of Rudraksha tree. The Rudraksha allowed the yogi to discern if a fruit or water in the wilderness of the jungle was fit to consume.

7.7 Outcome Measures of LOC

The difficulties in reliably measuring the level of consciousness notwithstanding, there are some straightforward ways to get a handle on LOC at least in the qualitative sense and these ways are amenable to experiential validation. The first among them is how we respond to external conditions. Changes in external conditions are unavoidable as they are part and parcel of life. If an individual remains unfettered (centered) in spite of the most favorable or unfavorable of external conditions, then the level of consciousness may be taken to be high. On the other hand if the same condition produces extreme positive or negative emotions, then much progress remains to be made. Here, when we speak of reactions to external conditions, we mean instant reactions, reflex reactions and not after we have had time to think how we should react. For example, if we stub our toe, what words come out of our mouth? If someone cuts into your lane nearly causing an accident, what is your instant reaction? This idea gives a great way to track our own progress on the scale of consciousness. Figure 7.6 depicts the two conditions.

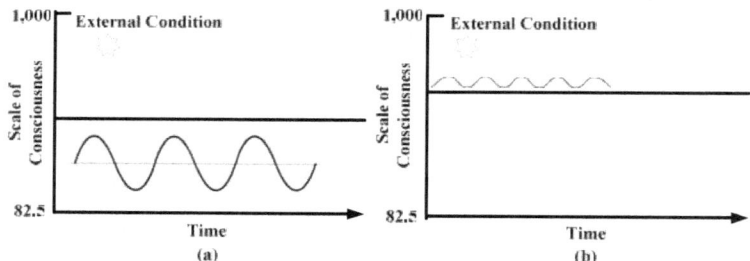

Figure 7.6. Influence of External Condition on Internal Conditions, Happiness

Not long ago, the first author presented a lecture on Science of True Happiness to a senior class of Economics majors in the School of Business at the University of Louisville. Friend and colleague Prof. Babu Nahata teaches a mandatory class to seniors in their department with the title of Economics of Happiness. In their discipline apparently there is something called *Easterlin paradox*, a phrase coined after Prof. Easterlin discovered that during 1950s and 1990s the self-reported index of wellness/happiness was either stagnant or had declined although income levels were steadily rising. In the seminar, the thirteen students were asked to rate their own index of happiness on a scale of 1 to 5 and they gave themselves an average rating of 3.09. The issue of reactions to external conditions wasn't deliberately made clear to them. Had they been aware when we speak of reaction to external conditions we mean instantaneous reaction, the average rating would have been far lower.

This idea makes it possible to identify someone who is at a very high level of consciousness. Such an individual is also recognizable by the spontaneous affection shown by people, animals, bird, and butterflies.

To summarize

Our goal is to rise on the scale of consciousness and for this a scale of consciousness and a way to measure it are needed so we may track progress. We have discussed several methods of measuring the state of consciousness and the uncertainties in these measurement methods. These ideas and concepts will be helpful as we progress in our quest towards wholesome excellence.

Further Reading

[1] Deshpande, P. B. and Kulkarni, B. D., The Brahma Uncertainty Principle, *Journal of Consciousness Exploration & Research*, Vol. 3, No. 2, February 2012.

[2]   Hawkins, David, R., *Qualitative and Quantitative Analysis and Calibration of the Level of Human Consciousness*, Veritas Publishing, W. Sedona, AZ 1995.

[3]   Monte, Daniel A., et al., Muscle Test Comparisons of Congruent and Incongruent Self-Referential Statements, Perceptive and Motor Skills, 88, 1999 pp. 1019-1028.

CHAPTER 8
Bioenergy Field Measurements

Early in the book, we learned that the nothingness of the void is (Brahmanic) consciousness. Humans also have personal (Atmanic) consciousness and the two are connected with a field of energy, bioenergy to be more precise, that has enormous intelligence. Tapping into this field brings many benefits as we will see in the ensuing chapters. Since bioenergy is so important, it is important to be able to measure it so that we may track our progress.

One of the outstanding people to whom this monograph is dedicated is Prof. Konstantin Korotkov in large measure because of his breakthrough work in the measurement of human bioenergy field with a scientific device. In the mid-nineties Konstantin developed a scientific device based on the principle of GDV (gas discharge visualization) which uses the ancient Chinese system of energy meridians for measuring the bioenergy of living organisms and the environment. The device provides noninvasive, painless and almost immediate evaluation which can highlight potential abnormalities prior to even the earliest symptoms of an underlying condition. This is because our bioenergy field is the first to be disrupted well before the symptoms of a disease are manifested in the physical body.

8.1 Principles of Gas Discharge Visualization

GDV utilizes a weak, completely painless electric current applied to the fingertips of all ten fingers one at a time for less than a millisecond. The body's response to this stimulus is the formation of a variation of "electron cloud" composed of light energy, photons. The electronic "glow" of this discharge, invisible to the human eye is captured by an optical CCD camera system and then translated into a digital computer file. The data from each test is converted into a unique "Photonic Profile", which is compared to the database of hundreds of thousands of records using 55 distinct parametric discriminates and charted so that they are available for discussion and analysis. A graph of the findings is presented as a two-dimensional image. To study these images, fractal, matrix and various algorithmic techniques are linked and analyzed. In addition, the system provides instant graphical representation to provide easy reference and interpretation. For further clarification, a graphical representation is generated, placing the indicators within the outline of the human form for ease of explanation and discussion. For a more in-depth understanding of GDV, the reader is referred to the papers listed at the end of the chapter. GDV has been in the market for over fifteen years and has received registration as a routine medical diagnostic device by the Russian Ministry of Health upon recommendation of the Russian Academy of Sciences.

A schematic of a GDV device named Bio-Well is shown in Figure 8.1. The GDV device has numerous applications in the field of medicine and sports. It can determine the

Figure 8.1 Bio-Well GDV Device

physiological and psycho-emotional state of a human and when combined with another indicator such as an aura photograph, the spiritual state of a human being. The GDV provides several parameters that are indicative of the physiological and psycho-emotional state: (1) Stress level, (2) Bioenergy intensity, (3) Normality of various organs and systems, and (4) Sate of the Chakras. These parameters allow aspirants to gage the extent of progress they are making with their practices such as Yoga, Pranayam, meditation, medical interventions, etc.

A special software environment allows for the processing and analyzing BIO-grams oriented towards the work in different problem domains. Adaptation for a particular assessment is performed through a combination of optimal operations from the library for the given problem domain, selection of corresponding procedures, and (or) selection of optimal threshold values.

8.2 Computational Algorithms in Bio-Well

The following main algorithms are included in the library:

Pseudo-coloring. For visual estimation of the image, there are several algorithms of pseudo-coloring, oriented towards marking out several peculiarities of BIO -grams. The following **Intensity palette** is most commonly used. In this processing, image points are colored in one of eight colors. The brightest glow points are colored in the shades of blue, less bright points are colored in the shades of red. Points are colored in yellow when the intensity is higher than the noise level, but lower than the base noise level for the given frame. All image points removed by noise filtration are shown as white background. Special programs are designed for the calculation of the following BIO-gram parameters: ***Total image area (S)****: the number of pixels in the image having brightness above the threshold.* ***Average Intensity (I)*** is an evaluation of the Intensity spectrum for the particular BIO-gram. **Entropy (Entr)** of the image is calculated in accordance with non-linear algorithm, presented in Korotkov (2012). The **Energy (E)** of light emitted by the subject is equal to:

$$E = k \, S*I \; (Joules) \qquad (7.3)$$

Where k is a numerical coefficient depending on spectral parameters of the particular CCD camera. For the GDV instruments $k = 2*10^{-4}$.

8.3 Chakras and Interpretation

In yogic thinking, the human system is composed of five sheaths: (1) Annamaya Kosha – Food body, (2) Pranamaya Kosha – life-force or pranic energy sheath, (3) Manomaya Kosha – sheath of rational mind, (4) Dyanamaya Kosha –

sheath of psychic impressions, and (5) Anandamaya Kosha – Blissful sheath. The first, Annamaya Kosha, is what we recognize as the physical body. The rest are energy sheaths. Yogis assert that there is abundant energy in the cosmos. We only draw 10% of the energy or life-force via the food we eat, another 20% from the air we breathe, and the rest by the seven energy centers called chakras and supplied to the body via 7,200,000 energy channels called Nadis. There are seven major chakras: (1) Muladhar, (2) Swadhisthan, (3) Manipur, (4) Anahat, (5) Vishuddhi, (6) Ajna, and (7) Sahasrar. The glow of the various sectors of the fingers of each hand correlate with a specific chakra. These relationships are shown in Figure 8.2.

In working with chakras, two things are important: Size, indicative of energy, Joules, and Alignment along the vertical central line. Ideally, all seven chakras need to be of optimal size meaning optimal energy, joules and perfectly aligned along the central line. When the finger sectors of the left hand and the right hand both give identical *and* optimal values of energy then they are perfect in size and perfectly aligned along the central line. The smaller the sizes, the more problematic the condition. Also, the more different the energy levels of chakras as determined by the fingers of the right hand versus the left hand, further they will be to the left or the right of the center. The more the misalignment, the more problematic the condition. On the basis of thousands of individual records, Konstantin and associates developed

76 | *Chapter 8. Bioenergy Field Measurements*

the optimal sizes of each of the seven chakras. The optimal energy value of each chakra is 5.0 joules.

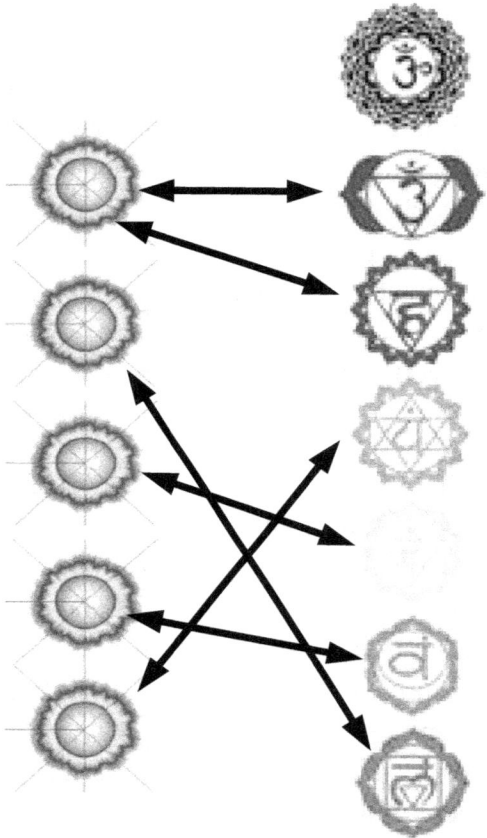

Figure 8.2 Correlations between Finger Sectors and Chakras (Source, Korotkov, 2002)

Healthy and Unwell Condition. The upper two images in Figure 8.3 show the bioenergy field and chakras of a physiologically fit and emotionally stable individual. Contrast this with the same in the lower two figures. The differences are obvious.

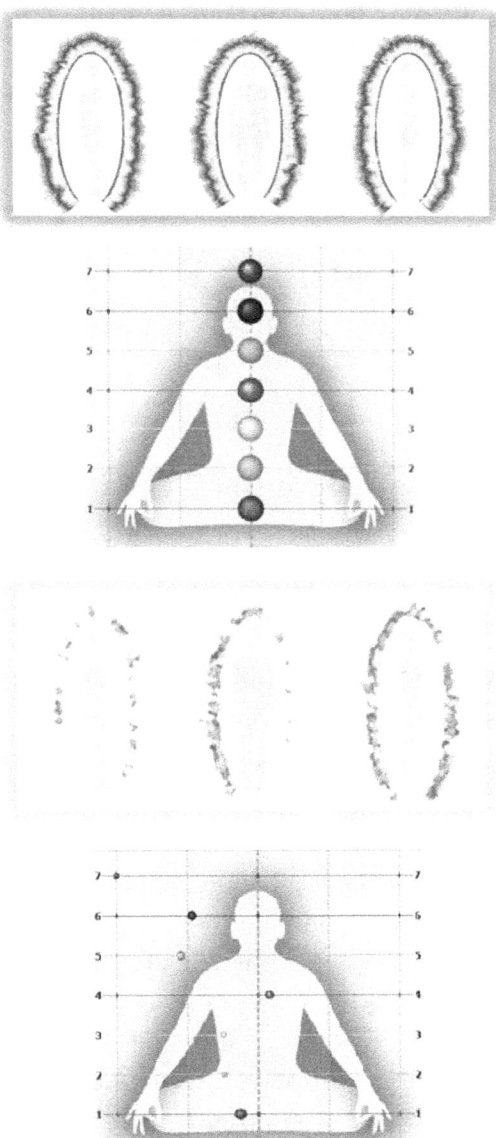

Figure 8.3 Bioenergy Field, Chakras of a Healthy and Unwell Individual

8.4 Normal Energy Ranges (Orlov, 2014)

Table 8.1 shows the normal ranges for the bioenergy values of systems and organs in joules.

Table 8.1. Bio-Well Energy Values

No.	Energy	Conclusion
1	0 - 1.99	Very low
2	2.0-3.99	Low
3	4.0-5.99	Normal
4	6.0-7.99	Increased
5	8.0 - ….	High

These ranges were established by scrutinizing the bioenergy data of tens of thousands of apparently healthy individuals. This brings out a distinguishing feature of the GDV approach. A standard medical device such as CT scan or an MRI provides the diagnostics of the specific patient under scrutiny. Unlike the standard approach, the GDV is based on statistics. It answers the question, compared to tens of thousands of apparently healthy individuals, where does the subject stand with a high probability, say 95%.

Our current health condition is the cumulative effect of our past energy field while our current energy field is predictive of our future health condition. For this reason, disruption in our energy field is a wakeup call for action.

8.5 Working with the GDV Device

Working with the GDV device is simple and straight forward but the interpretation of the results requires specialized training. The equipment required includes the Bio-Well device, connecting cable to connect it to the laptop or PC, a calibrating device for device calibration, and Bio-Well software installed on the computer. Bio-Well must be calibrated on a regular basis. To get started, the device is connected to the USB port of the computer and the software is launched. Then, the name of the person whose bioenergy is to be measured is registered. Next, the full scan button is pressed which brings up ten boxes, one for each finger. Now, the subject inserts the finger through an opening in the device and with gentle pressure rests the pulp of the finger inserted on the glass electrode. The operator presses the Scan button and the device captures the glow from that finger. Care is taken to insure that the scanned image of the finger glow on the screen is as close to a circle as possible and that the image is more or less centered in the square box of each finger. When all ten fingers are scanned, the operator pushes the analyze button and moments later the results are displayed on the computer screen.

Let us take an example: Figure 8.4(a) depicts the images of the ten fingers of Dmitry Orlov taken on September 22, 2014. Dmitry is General Manager of Bio Well Company. Figure 8.4(b) shows the energy field. Figure 8.4(c) shows stress level, energy level, and balance. Figure 8.4(d) depicts the energy status of this individual while Figure 8.4(e) shows the chakras. Dmitry's bioenergy measurements are excellent.

Chapter 8. Bioenergy Field Measurements

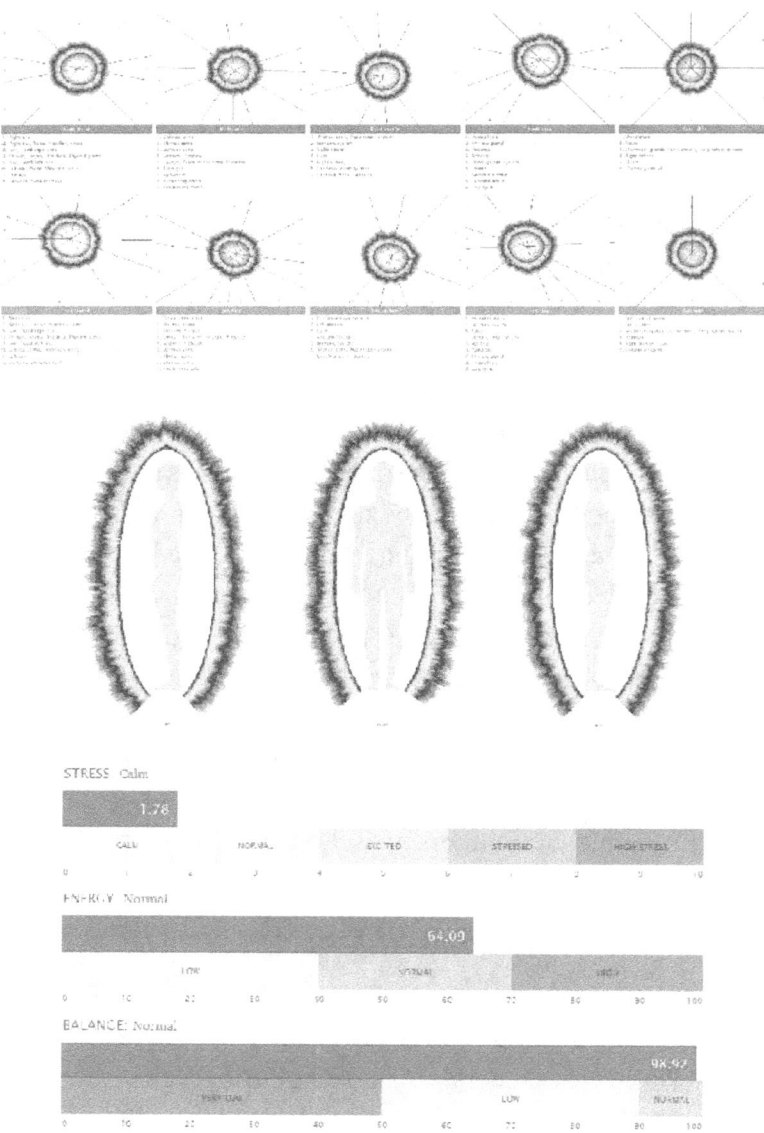

Figure 8.4(a) Finger Images, (b) Energy Field (Middle), (c) Stress, Energy, Balance (Bottom)

81 | Chapter 8. Bioenergy Field Measurements

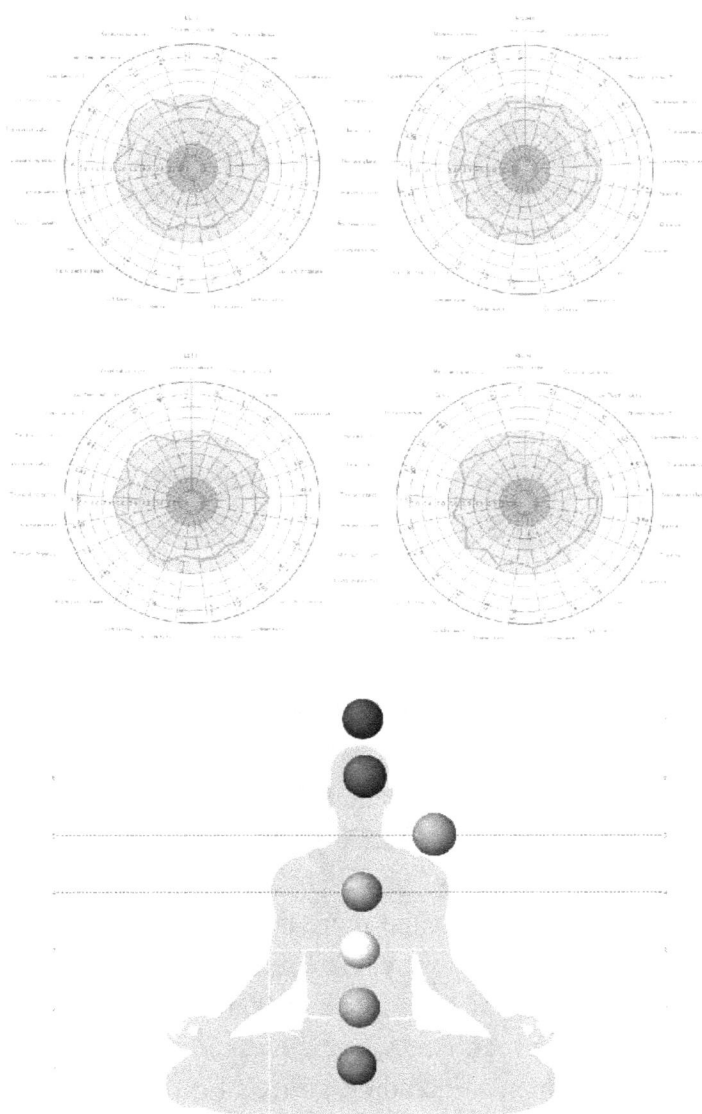

Figure 8.4(d) Health Status (e) Energy Status (Middle), (f) Chakras (Bottom)

In this context, the work of Elizabeth Blackburn, PhD assumes significance. Dr. Blackburn and associates discovered in the seventies that the tips of chromosomes called telomeres in the nucleus of our cells act as caps to protect the ends of our chromosomes each time our cells are divided and the DNA copied. They also discovered that an enzyme called telomerase can protect and rebuild telomeres. As we age, telomerase levels reduce and telomeres dwindle and when they get too short, our cells malfunction and lose their ability to divide and this is a key process that contributes to aging. This work eventually earned Dr. Blackburn the Nobel Prize in physiology and medicine in 2009 and more recently the title of Medicine Buddha from fellow Nobel laureate, HH Dalai Lama (www.cnn.com, 2014).

Blackburn and her colleague Elissa Epel at the University of California San Francisco collaborated showing that telomerase levels and telomeres length are strongly correlated with stress levels and that they affect aging. For their project the team meticulously recruited fifty-eight women who were caring for their chronically ill children. The results showed that the more stressed the women said they were, the shorter were their telomeres and lower the telomerase levels (Epel, et al., 2004). This finding is significant since high stress levels are known to contribute to 80% of ailments including cancer says the American Medical Association.

Prof. Blackburn's approach requires the analysis of blood samples in a specialized pathological laboratory for telomere length and telomerase level estimated to cost $500 or more per sample. Bioenergy measurements on the other hand are noninvasive, painless, cost effective, and take only a couple of minutes to complete. There is no single study as yet which proves that when the bioenergy field is disrupted, the telomere length and telomerase levels are compromised.

To summarize

In the previous chapter we discussed several methods of measuring the level of consciousness and the uncertainties in these measurement methods. The optimal chakra sizes and locations also might be indicative of a high level of consciousness but to distinguish such individuals from ones who are merely healthy and centered, another measurement such as aura photography might be required. The bioenergy parameters indicate the physiological and psychoemotional state and when combined with the Aura measurement may indicate our level of consciousness.

Further Reading

1. Blackburn, Elizabeth on CNN.COM July 10, 2014 http://www.cnn.com/health/can-meditation-really-slow-aging/).
2. Chez, Ronald, A., Ed., Proceedings: Measuring the Human Energy Field – State of the Science, The Gerontology Research Center, National Institute on Aging, National Institute of Health, Baltimore, MD April 17 - 18, 2002.
3. Blackburn, Elizabeth and Epel, Elissa, Telomere and Adversity - Too Toxic to Ignore, Nature, 490, 11 October 2012 pp. 169-171.

4 Epel, Elissa, et al., Accelerated Telomere Shortening in Response to Life Stress, Proceedings of the National Academy of Sciences, 101, 49, December 2004. pp. 17312-17315.
5 Jakovleva E., Korotkov K., Electrophotonic Analysis in Medicine. GDV Bioelectrography research. 2013. 160 p. Amazon.com.
6 Korotkov K.G., Matravers P, Orlov D.V., Williams B.O. Application of Electrophoton Capture (EPC) Analysis Based on Gas Discharge Visualization (GDV) Technique in Medicine: A Systematic Review. The J of Alternative and Complementary Medicine. January 2010, 16, 1, pp.13-25.
7 Korotkov K.G., Energy Fields Electrophotonic Analysis in Humans and Nature, 2012. 240 p. e-book: Amazon.com.
8 Korotkov K. and Orlov D., Analysis of Stimulated Electrophotonic Glow of Liquids, V 2, 2010 (www.WaterJournal.org).
9 Korotkov K., Korotkin D. Concentration Dependence of Gas Discharge Around Drops of Inorganic Electrolytes. J of Applied Physics, 2001, 89, 9, 4732-4737.
10 Orlov, Dmitry, Private Communication, 2014.
11 Pehek J. O., Kyler, H. J., and Foust, D. L., Image Modulation in Corona Discharge Photography, Science, Vol. 194, 263 – 270, October 1976.

CHAPTER 9
Discovering something within ourselves that can affect us

The quest to raise our level of consciousness, internal excellence, is an internal search and therefore it is necessary to find something within ourselves that has an effect on our own selves. Furthermore, whatever evidence we might discover must be so strong as to be convincing to the deepest recesses of our hearts and minds. Then progress would be within our reach. Most readers today are rational minded and so such an inquiry must be supported by scientific experimentation.

Some of the greatest scientific minds of our time had come tantalizingly close to unraveling the mystery of that within us which has an effect on ourselves but couldn't quite connect the dots principally because the path-breaking DNA work of Nobel Laureates Watson and Crick had not yet been done. For example, Nikola Tesla is reported to have stated in early twentieth century, *"If you wish to understand the universe, think of energy, frequency, vibration"*. On another occasion he said, *"The day science begins to study non-physical phenomena, it will make more progress in one decade than in all the previous centuries of its existence"*.

Max Planck is quoted as saying, '*All matter originates only by virtue of a force. We must assume behind this force the existence of a conscious and intelligent mind. This mind is the matrix of all matter*' (Braden, 2007). And Albert Einstein once reportedly said, '*A human being is part of the whole called by us universe, a part limited in time and space. He experiences himself, his thoughts, his feelings as something separated from the rest – A kind of optical delusion of his consciousness. This delusion is kind of like prison for us, restricting us to our personal desires and affection for a few persons nearest to us. Our task must be to free ourselves from this prison by widening our circle of compassion to embrace all living creatures and the whole nature in its beauty*'. These renowned scientists had come tantalizing close to unraveling the mystery.

Western scientists have made phenomenal progress on this front in recent decades. In The Divine Matrix (Hay House Publishers, 2009), the New York Times best-selling author Gregg Braden presents several experiments of western scientists during 1993–2000 that are a game changer. They encompass three topics: (1) Evidence that there is a form of energy heretofore unrecognized which affects us in a fundamental way, (2) Evidence that all of us are connected even though not physically linked, (3) Evidence that is something within ourselves that has an impact on us.

9.1 Field of Energy that Affects our DNA

There is experimental evidence suggesting the presence of an energy field in the universe heretofore unrecognized that

Chapter 9. Discovering something within ourselves

has an effect on our DNA. Russian scientists Vladimir Poponin, Peter Gariaev, and associates conducted an experiment in Russia to study the effect of photon particles on human DNA. They first studied the contents of an evacuated chamber and found that the chamber contained photon particles that were randomly scattered everywhere as in Figure 9.1(Left), not an unexpected observation. Next, they placed human DNA inside the chamber and examined the contents again. Now, the photon particles arranged themselves around the DNA (Figure 9.1(Center). Then, they removed the DNA only to discover that the photon particles remained ordered as though the DNA was still present instead of reverting to the random configuration (Figure 9.1 (Right). No change of any kind is possible without energy

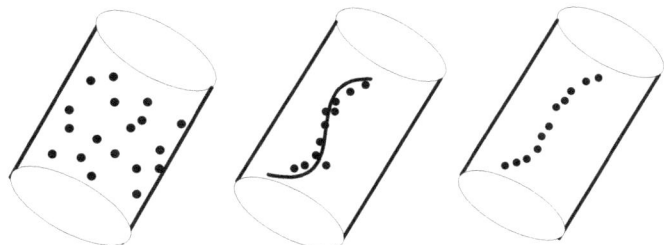

Figure 9.1 Poponin Experiments

and so this experiment reveals the presence of a field of energy that can bring about a change in human DNA. The results depicted in Figure 9.1 are an adaption of the figures in the Divine Matrix (Braden, 2009).

Dr. Rollin McCraty, Executive Vice president and Director of Research at the Institute for the HeartMath in Boulder Creek, California, mentioned to the first author that they had reproduced these results when Poponin was at the Institute on a visiting assignment (McCraty, 2013).

9.2 Everything is Connected to Everything Else

In unraveling the mystery of the beginning of the universe, we saw that the size of the universe was the Planck length (10^{-33} cm in diameter) at the moment of the Big Bang. Everything was connected to everything else then. Out of that nothingness came out Amanda Gefter's something, the universe. The beauty is that everything in the universe remains connected to everything else even though not physically linked. Recognizing this connectedness is a key to progress.

The idea of connectedness has been known since ancient times. The notion of Indra's Net from Mahayana Buddhism sheds some light: '*Far away in the heavenly abode of the great god Indra, there is a wonderful net that stretches out infinitely in all directions. There is a single glittering jewel in each "eye" of the net, and since the net itself is infinite in dimension, so are the jewels. Looking closely at any one of these jewels will reveal that in its polished surface are reflected all the other jewels in the net. Not only that, but each of the jewels reflected in this one jewel is also reflecting all the other jewels*'. A pictorial depiction of the Indra's Net is shown in Figure 9.2.

There are many day-to-day examples of connectedness. Reflect on how a mother knows that her infant child is hungry, how a sibling among a set of twins living far away knows what the other is thinking, etc. A scientific example

Chapter 9. Discovering something within ourselves

Figure 9.2 Indra's Net (Source: http://en.wikipedia.org/wiki/Indra%27s_net; Copyleft - Free Software Foundation, Inc.)

involves an experiment Quantum Physicist Prof. Nicholas Gisin of the University of Geneva conducted which studied the behavior of photon particles. The experiment consisted of two 7-mile optical fiber channels. Pathways were provided at the outlet of each channel through which the photon particles could travel. A simplified schematic of the experimental setup is shown in Figure 9.3.

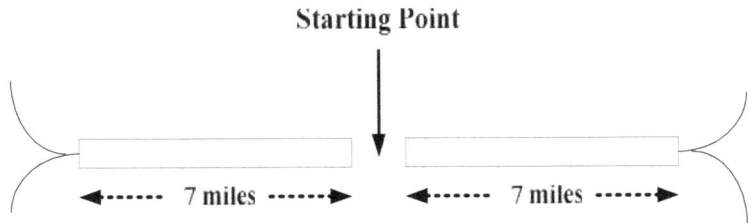

Figure 9.3 Quantum Entanglement Experiment

Now a photon particle was split in half to produce two identical twins. Then at the starting point the two particles were fired in the opposite directions so that when they arrived at the channel outlet they would be fourteen miles apart. When the particles arrived at their destination, each particle had a choice to choose one path or the other. The two particles made precisely the same choices and traveled the same path every time, again and again! This is an indication that the particles seemed to remain connected although no longer physically linked.

9.3 Effect of Emotions on DNA

In the Divine Matrix Gregg Braden presents the results of an experiment the US Army conducted in 1993 to study the possible impact of emotions on DNA. They collected a sample of tissue and DNA from a subject's mouth and located it in a different room in the building. Then, the subject was shown videos which were selected to evoke a spectrum of emotions. The researchers discovered that every time the subject experienced emotional peaks and valleys, his cells and DNA exhibited powerful electrical responses at the same instant although the subject and the DNA were separated by a distance measured in hundreds of feet. These results are shown in Figure 9.4.

Braden also reported that the senior US Army scientist who had designed the experiment had repeated the experiment when the subject and the DNA were 350 miles apart but the results were the same. Furthermore, the time difference

Chapter 9. Discovering something within ourselves

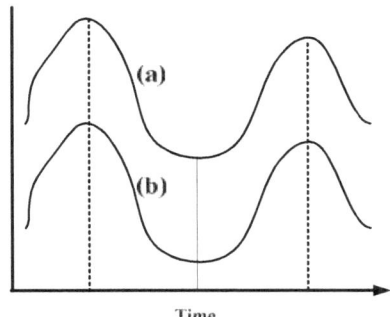

**Figure 9.4 Effect of Emotions on DNA
(a) Donor's Reactions, (b) DNA Response**

between the subject's emotions and the cell's response as measured by an atomic clock in Colorado was zero. In other words, the emotions were already at the destination the instant they were generated without a time lag. The remotely-located DNA acted as if it was still connected to the subject in some way. So what is it within ourselves that has an impact on ourselves? EMOTIONS. This finding strongly resonates with yogic thinking.

9.4 Effect of Coherence + Intention on DNA

Researchers at the Institute for HeartMath (IHM) conducted an experiment in 1995 to study the effect of coherence + intention on DNA placed in a beaker several feet away. They assigned the task to a group of five who were trained in achieving high coherence to focus on the placental DNA. With high coherence, which is associated with positive emotions – unconditional love, compassion, kindness, appreciation, etc., the team could intentionally wind or unwind the DNA. Figure 9.5 depicts an adaptation of IHM results.

Figure 9.5 With Coherence + Intention the Team could wind or unwind the DNA

9.5 Effect of Emotions on Others

Dr. Rollin McCraty of the Institute for HeartMath was kind enough to share the images in Figure 9.6 that reinforce the idea that emotions can affects others, in this case a horse named Tonopah and a pet dog named Mabel. The central areas in Figure 9.6(a) and (b) are when Ellen/Tonopah and Josh/Mabel are together, a time for affection; otherwise they are apart. The coherence is unmistakable. Dr. McCraty also shared an image shown in Figure 9.7 which shows the effect of positive and negative emotions on heart rate variability.

To Conclude

We have now discovered on the basis of scientific experimentation that there in fact is something within us that affects ourselves in a fundamental way and it is emotions.

93 | Chapter 9. Discovering something within ourselves

We also surmise that positive emotions (unconditional love, empathy, compassion, kindness) have life-supporting influence on us while negative emotions (anger, hostility, hatred, despair, etc.) have life-degrading influence. In the next chapter we will see how we could raise our level of consciousness using the ideas we have learned in this chapter.

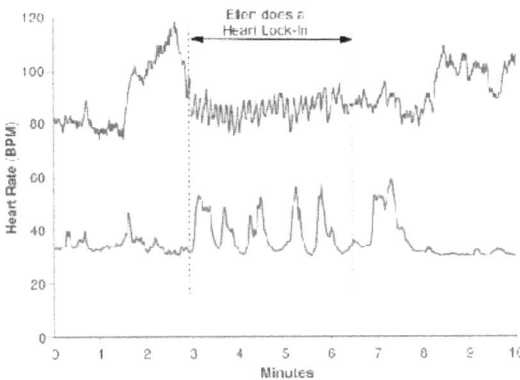

Figure 9.6(a) Ellen and Tonopah (Source, IHM)

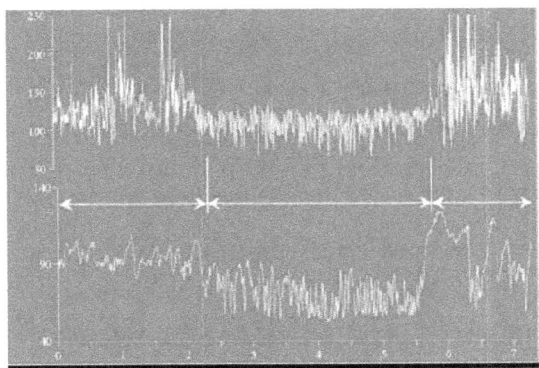

Figure 9.6(b) Josh and Mabel (Source, IHM)

Chapter 9. Discovering something within ourselves

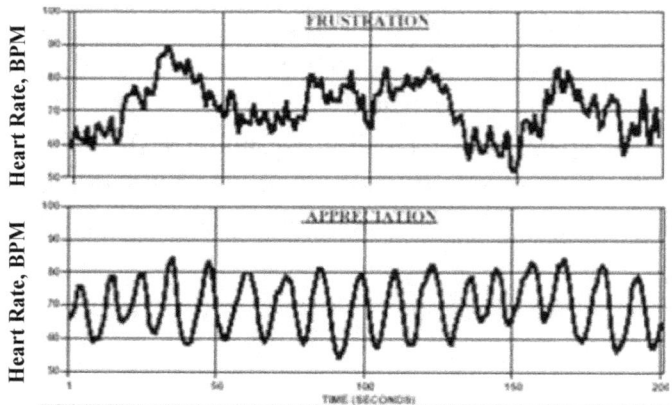

Figure 9.7 Effect of Positive and Negative Emotions on Heart Rate Variability (Source, Ref. 2, IHM)

Further Reading

1. **Braden, Gregg**, The Divine Matrix, Hay House Publishers, 2007.
2. **McCraty, R., Atkinson, M., and Tomasino, D.**, Science of the Heart, HeartMath Research Center, Publication No. 01-001, Institute for HeartMath, Boulder Creek, CA 2001.
3. **Poponin, Vladimir**, The DNA Phantom Effect: Direct Measurement of a New Field in a Vacuum Structure, http://www.bibliotecapleyades.net/ciencia/ciencia_genetica04.htm
4. **Rein, Glenn and McCraty, R.,** Structural Changes in Water and DNA Associated with a New Physiologically Measurable State, J. Scientific Exploration, 8, 3, 1994 pp. 438-439.

CHAPTER 10
Why We Get Sick

This chapter presents a yogic perspective on diseases followed by a modern physics perspective. The yogic perspective is an adaptation of Baba Shivanand Ji's discourses. You will see that this material resonates with Chapter 4 on the nature of consciousness. Once we have understood these concepts, it becomes easier to embrace the path forward for progress presented in the ensuing several chapters.

10.1 Yogic Perspective

Our body is made up of several subsystems: Respiratory system, endocrine system, cardiovascular system, urogenital system, digestive system, excretory system, etc. Associated with each subsystem are specific organs. For example, associated with the respiratory system are heart, lungs, etc. Urogenital system organs are kidneys, sexual organs, bladder, etc. Each organ is made up of tissues. Tissues in turn are made up of cells. Medical science knows that the cells in all the organs disintegrate into atoms and flow out to be completely replaced by new cells every so often. For example, the cells in the heart are replaced by new cells in a few months. Thus, after this amount of time, not a single old cell is present. Allegorically, our body is like a flowing river. If we dip a glass in the river and fill it with water at one instant and fill it again at another instant, the water in the two glasses will not be the same. The water in the first glass has travelled downstream and been replaced by the water coming from upstream. Now, suppose there is a specific type of defect in some part the body, say in the heart or heart-valve. The interesting question is how do these new cells know that the new cells at that particular spot must have exactly the same defect as the old cells? Take another example, suppose an individual has one normal kidney and one shrunken kidney. What technology do the cells know that enables them to produce exactly the defective cells required for the shrunken kidney and not healthy cells for a normal kidney?

Yogis have deciphered this mystery in ancient times through meditation. They say, just as a building has an architectural drawing, an electrical drawing, plumbing drawing, etc., the mind too is like a supercomputer having the complete mapping of every organ and system. If there is a diseased cell, deceased cell is born, if there is a normal cell, normal cell is born. Now, what is that mapping? What is that information?

What are cells made of? Of course, a nucleus and a gel-like substance called cytoplasm. These in turn are composed of chromosomes, nucleic acids; DNA and RNA, carbohydrates, proteins, lipids, etc. If we break down the cells further, they are made up of atoms. The question is, what characteristic of the atoms gives the specific character to matter? The answer

Chapter 10. Why We Get Sick

is, atomic configuration. For example, iron is iron and gold is gold because of their specific atomic configuration. Change the atomic configuration and the specific character of the matter will change. The mind is such an amazing super computer that it creates exactly the required atomic configuration. Where there was a diseased cell, exactly the same diseased cell is created. Now the next question is what is this super computer and where is it?

Science says that if all the atoms in the body are collected, they will only account for a tiny portion, say 0.1% for simplicity, of the space in the physical body. This means that in the 99.9% of the space in the human body there is nothing. It is empty space and this is applicable to all solid matter. Science does not know what is in the empty space but yogis suggest that the empty space houses vibrations that are directly responsible for our cellular structure. Quantum physics tells us that atoms are made up of subatomic particles. Atoms are not solid objects. They are made up of electrons, protons, and neutrons, i. e., energy, as are the subatomic particles. In a sense we are all beings of energy. Going into a meditative state, Yogis saw that beyond the subatomic particles are micro atomic particles and beyond the micro atomic particles there is the holographic memory of the individual continuously playing what is analogous to a three-dimensional film of what has happened in his life. Someone has given joy, someone has caused agony, etc. This film is such that it plays and replays continuously over and over creating more and more structures; two from one, four from two, and so on. This film, these vibrations, this energy controls the micro atomic particles which controls the subatomic particles which in turn controls the atomic particles, and finally the atomic configuration. From the atomic configuration is born the cellular structure. The link between the atomic configuration, cellular structure, and illnesses may be seen to be emerging.

But what is creating these vibrations? In yogic thinking, the human system is composed of five sheaths: (1) Annamaya Kosha – Food body, (2) Pranamaya Kosha – Body of life-force or pranic energy, (3) Manomaya Kosha – Body of rational mind, (4) Dyanamaya Kosha – Body of Intellect, and (5) Anandamaya Kosha – Blissful Body. The first sheath, Annamaya Kosha, is what we take as the physical body and although it may appear to be physical, we know that it too is composed of subatomic particles, i. e., energy. We know the Einstein's famous equation $E = mc^2$ or in vedic terminology, I am a being of light.

What happens in a specific Kosha is governed by the next Kosha higher up. Annamaya Kosha is the physical body the way we understand it. Yogis assert that there is abundant energy in the cosmos. We only draw 10% of the energy, or life force, via the food we eat, another 20% from the air we breathe, and the rest by the seven energy centers called chakras, energy meridians, and supplied to the body via 7,200,000 energy channels called Nadis which are the home of Pranamaya Kosha or the body of Pranic Energy. Inefficient breathing and improperly functioning chakras means that we are deficient in the life-force energy.

Chapter 10. Why We Get Sick

Manomaya Kosha is where thoughts and emotions are processed. Yogis suggest that the mind body is what creates the vibrations, energy, in the empty space. What happens in the Manomaya Kosha is governed by what is in the Dyanamaya Kosha. Dyanamaya Kosha has imprinted in it the psychic impressions created by our karmas, our past actions. In Yogic thinking, there are three types of karmas: Sancheet Karma, the infinite amount of karmas accumulated from past lives, Prarabaddha Karma, the karmas that we are born with, and Agama Karma, the karmas which we accumulate in this life by our actions from early childhood to the present age. Our actions directly correlate with our emotions: Positive emotions generate good actions or good karma while negative emotions, bad actions or bad karma. Now, the importance of positive emotions for good health may be seen to be emerging.

So, why do we get sick? The yogic explanation should now be clear. One source of the problem is the food we eat, the second is the inefficient capture of life-force energy, and the third and perhaps the most important is the psychic impressions imprinted in the Dyanamaya Kosha due to our negative emotions in this life and negative karmas from past lives. All three factors influence the energy in the empty space and consequently the atomic configuration and therefore, cellular structure. It is with these ideas in mind that Patanjali (~ 500 bce) must have come up with the eight-fold Yoga system: Yama and Niyama for ethical living, Asanas for external subsystems – spine, muscles, joints, etc., Pranayama for maximizing the intake of life-force energy for internal organs and subsystems, and Pratyahara for the withdrawal of sense organs from sense objects. The last three are increasingly deeper levels of meditation. Swami Vivekananda introduced Yoga to America over a hundred years ago but the bone-bending exercises that have come to be known as Yoga (Asanas) is a suboptimal use of Yoga.

10.2 Nobel Laureate's Breakthrough Work

The Internet account of a human body tells us that each body has trillions of cells, the estimates varying greatly because of the varying sizes and densities. Each cell has a nucleus which contains 46 chromosomes which come as 23 pairs; 22 pairs are called autosomes and the remaining pair is called sex chromosome - X, X for females and X, Y for males. Between the nucleus and the cell wall is cytoplasm which is comprised of cytosol, a gel-like substance (see Figure 10.1).

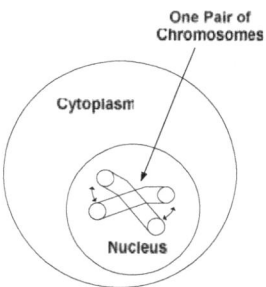

Figure 10.1. Diagram of a Cell

Cytosol makes up about 70% of the cell volume and is composed of water, salts and organic molecules (Wikipedia). Cells divide, mature, and die, and therefore every so often, a human body has all new cells.

Chapter 10. Why We Get Sick

Elizabeth Blackburn and associates at UCSF discovered in the seventies that the tips of human chromosomes called telomeres act as caps to protect the ends of our chromosomes each time our cells are divided and the DNA is copied. They also discovered that an enzyme called telomerase can protect and rebuild telomeres. As we age, telomeres dwindle and when they get too short, our cells malfunction and lose their ability to divide and this is a key process that contributes to aging. This work eventually earned Dr. Blackburn the 2009 Nobel Prize in physiology and medicine.

Elissa Epel subsequently collaborated with Blackburn showing that telomerase levels and telomeres length are strongly correlated with stress levels and that they affect aging. For their project the team meticulously recruited fifty-eight women who were caring for their chronically ill children. The results showed that the more stressed the women said they were, the shorter were their telomeres and lower the telomerase levels (Epel, et al., 2004). This finding is significant since high stress levels are known to contribute to a large number of ailments including cancer. Yogis say that 100% of the diseases are due to stress which result from negative psychic impressions in the Dyanamaya Kosha. As an illustration, Figure 10.2 depicts the Bioenergy field of an individual carrying an exceptionally high level of stress and the state of the chakras, courtesy of Prof. Konstantin Korotkov. The depiction is alarming and an urgent call for action.

102 | *Chapter 10. Why We Get Sick*

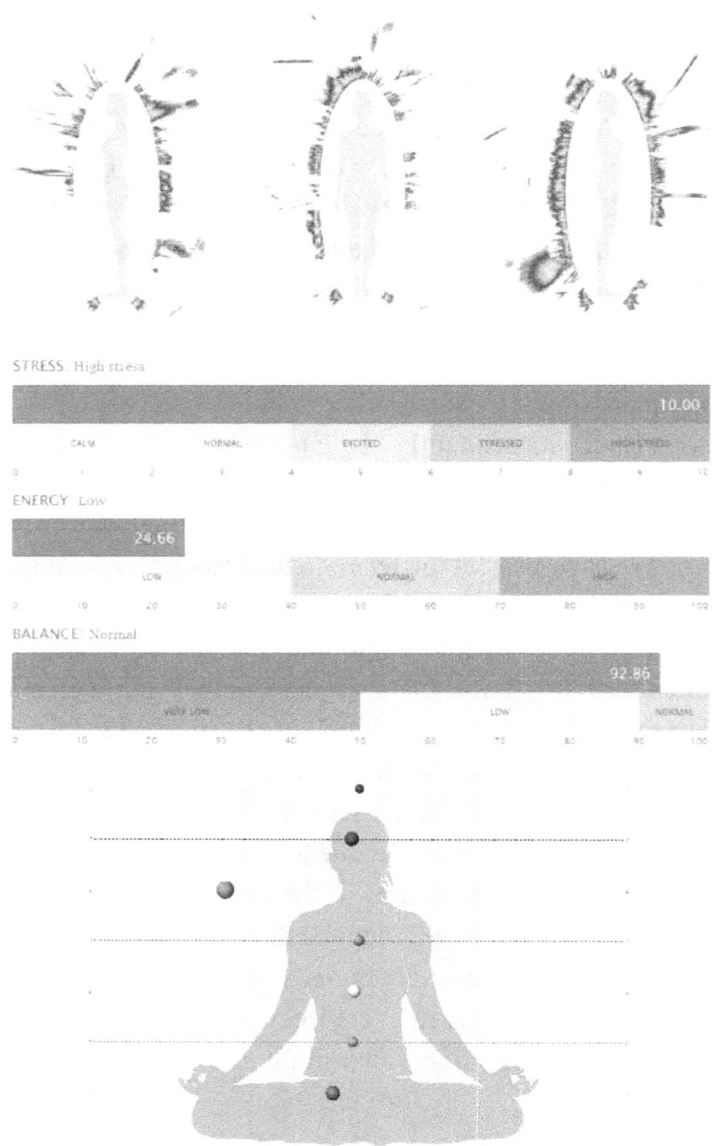

Figure 10.2. Bioenergy Field of a Stressed Individual

Chapter 10. Why We Get Sick

10.3 Quantum Mechanical Perspective on Health

In order to understand the quantum mechanical perspective on health, we have to address the basic problem of how consciousness, specifically the focus of attention of consciousness, is connected to physical phenomena, like physical health or illness of a body. There are two key ideas that can help us understand this connection:

1. The normal flow of energy in the world,

2. The quantum state of potentiality as constructed from an action principle.

There is no other place to begin except with cosmology, so let's begin with the usual starting point, the big bang event. We now know from observational evidence that the "bang" in the big bang is an actual explosion that is driven by the accelerated or exponential expansion of space. The two pieces of evidence for this expansion are measurements of the cosmic background radiation supporting the idea of inflationary cosmology and the current observed accelerated expansion of the universe as measured by the accelerated rate at which distant galaxies are moving away from us. The distant galaxies are moving away from us faster the farther out we look as though they repel each other. This repulsive force is called the force of dark energy, and is like a kind of anti-gravity. Things appear to move away from us faster the farther out we look in space due to the exponential expansion of space, which accelerates away from the central point of view of the observer. In relativity theory, dark energy is understood as a cosmological constant Λ.

Inflationary cosmology hypothesizes that Λ was about equal to 1 at the time of the big bang event while the current measured value of Λ is about 10^{-123}. Inflationary cosmology also hypothesizes that Λ changes in value through some kind of a phase transition, which is like a process of burning as a state of high potential energy transitions into a state of lower potential energy. There is some kind of a potential barrier separating the state of higher potential energy (often called a false vacuum) from the state of lower potential energy, and this potential barrier gives rise to a meta-stable state. The transition to the lower energy state occurs through a quantum tunneling event through the barrier and is like a process of burning that burns away dark energy. As the system burns and settles into a lower energy state, heat is radiated away. As the dark energy burns away, the value of Λ decreases.

This process of burning away the dark energy drives the normal flow of energy in the world. The mystery of this process is in the initial high value of Λ that occurred at the time of the big bang event giving rise to the accelerated or exponential expansion of space from the big bang. The reason this expansion ties in with consciousness is the nature of a cosmic horizon that arises from the accelerated expansion of space. To understand the cosmic horizon it is necessary to discuss the principle of equivalence, which is about the accelerated frame of reference of an observer that follows an accelerated worldline through space-time.

The cosmic horizon is a bounding surface of space surrounding the observer at the central point of view. The horizon is as far out in space as the observer at the central point of view can see things in space due to the limitation of the speed of light. At the cosmic horizon things appear to move away from the observer at the speed of light, and so nothing is observable beyond the horizon. This limitation in observations is due to the accelerated expansion of space away from the central point of view of the observer. This may seem weird but the point of singularity of the big bang event is the central point of view of the observer.

The existence of a cosmic horizon leads to the one-world-per-observer paradigm of modern cosmology. Amanda Gefter (2012) has written about this paradigm in her essay on Cosmic Solipsism. Her conclusions are based on recent developments in physics, including the nature of Hawking radiation, the holographic principle, horizontal complementarity, and the effects of a cosmological constant. The one-world-per-observer paradigm tells us that each observer has its own world which is ultimately limited by its own cosmic horizon. The best way to understand this is in terms of the holographic principle. All the fundamental quantized bits of information that ultimately define everything observable in the observer's world are ultimately encoded on its cosmic horizon, which is only a bounding surface of space that surrounds the observer at the central point of view. The encoding of bits of information on a two dimensional surface for whatever is perceived in the three dimensional space bounded by that surface is the nature of a hologram.

Different observers are able to share a consensual reality with one another because the different cosmic horizons can overlap in the sense of a Venn diagram. The bits of information encoded on each surface become entangled together in the sense of quantum entanglement and there is a sharing of information. By this mechanism the world of each observer can share information with the worlds of many other observers and so many different observers can share a consensual reality together. This entanglement of the worlds of many different observers has a nice metaphor in the net of Indra mentioned in Chapter 9.

Different observers, each at the central point of view of its own cosmic horizon, not only share information, but they also share in the normal flow of energy. This is easiest to see with thermodynamic concepts. The radius of the cosmic horizon is determined in relativity theory from the value of the cosmological constant as $(R/\ell)^2 = 3/\Lambda$, where ℓ is the Planck length. At the time of the big bang event Λ is about 1, and R is about a Planck length. As Λ decreases in value, R inflates in size to its current value of about 10^{62} Planck lengths or 15 billion light years.

The reason Λ decreases in value is because dark energy burns away. This burning away of dark energy drives the normal flow of energy in the world of each observer. To see this we use the Hawking calculation for the temperature of the horizon $kT = \hbar c/2\pi R$. At the time of the big bang, the horizon temperature was about 10^{32} degrees Kelvin, and as the horizon inflates in size, its temperature decreases. This temperature gradient drives the normal flow of energy.

Chapter 10. Why We Get Sick

As the dark energy burns away, heat is radiated away and tends to flow from the very hot big bang event to all colder states of the world as defined by an inflated cosmic horizon. This not only drives the normal flow of energy in the observer's world, but also in the consensual reality shared by many different observers. This normal flow of energy is driven by the accelerated expansion of space itself from the big bang event, which decelerates as dark energy burns away. Space is expanding away from the central point of view of the observer at an accelerated rate, but that acceleration slows down as the dark energy burns away.

This explains the normal flow of energy in the observer's world in the sense of the second law of thermodynamics. The mystery of this normal flow of energy is in the mystery of the high value of the cosmological constant at the time of the big bang event. The normal evolution of the world, and the normal flow of energy that drives that evolution, can be understood in terms of the burning away of dark energy and the flow of heat from the very hot big bang event to all colder states of the world arising with inflation of the cosmic horizon. The analogy of the flow of a river for the flow of energy is OK provided it is understood that the flow of energy isn't driven by the force of gravity but by the force of anti-gravity which becomes weaker over the course of time as Λ decreases in value.

These ideas allow us to understand the normal flow of energy but how does this flow of energy connect to how consciousness affects physical reality? We have to understand the holographic principle in terms of the action principle and a quantum state of potentiality. A quantum state of potentiality is only a sum over all possible configuration states of information that describe everything that can possibly appear to happen in the observer's world. The holographic principle tells us that those configuration states of information are defined on the bounding surface of space surrounding the observer at the central point of view, like a cosmic horizon. The bounding surface acts as a holographic screen. Each fundamental quantized bit of information is encoded on the screen, with one bit of information encoded per pixel on the screen. A bit of information is encoded in a binary code of 1's and 0's, which in quantum theory is understood in the sense of a spin ½ variable that can only point up or down, like a switch. The size of a pixel is about a Planck area. For a bounding surface with a radius R and a surface area $A = 4\pi R^2$, the total number of bits of information encoded is $n = A/4\ell^2$. A quantum state of potentiality is only a sum over all possible ways in which these bits of information can become encoded on the screen, which is a sum over all possible configuration states of information.

The principle of equivalence tells us that the bounding surface is only an event horizon that arises because the observer is in an accelerated frame of reference. That observer follows an accelerated worldline through space and time. The holographic principle tells us that this perceived space and time is holographically projected from the observer's holographic screen to the central point of view of the observer in terms of the spatial relationships between the objects perceived in space by the observer over a sequence

Chapter 10. Why We Get Sick

of events, just like the images projected to an observer from a computer screen over a sequence of screen outputs.

The holographic principle is a duality that relates the nature of the objects we perceive in three dimensional space to the bits of information encoded on the two dimensional bounding surface of that space. All the fundamental quantized bits of information are encoded on the bounding surface, and the objects perceived in three dimensional space are like a holographic projection of images to the central point of view of the observer. The holographic principle is weird since those perceivable objects in space even include the nature of elementary particles. Every object perceived in space, from an elementary particle to a macroscopic body, is like a projection of images from a holographic screen to the central point of view of an observer.

To make sense of this situation, we have to understand that each observational event is like a screen output from the observer's holographic screen to the central point of view of the observer. With each screen output, a particular configuration state of information is displayed on the observer's screen. The quantum state of potentiality characterizing the observer's screen is only a sum over all possible configuration states of information, but in any given screen output, a particular configuration state is actually displayed on the screen. Quantum theory has a name for this phenomena and it is called a quantum state reduction.

The other way to understand the quantum state of potentiality is as a sum over all possible paths, but what

110 | Chapter 10. Why We Get Sick

exactly do we mean by a path? A path is a worldline followed by an observer through space and time. Every observational event on the observer's worldline is like a screen output from the observer's holographic screen to the central point of view of the observer. The space-time geometry that characterizes the observer's frame of reference is holographically projected from the screen. That space-time geometry only has one invariant measure of length, called the proper time, which is the geometrical length of the observer's worldline.

In relativity theory we write the geometrical length of the worldline, $\tau = \int ds$, in terms of the metric as $ds^2 = g_{\mu\nu} dx^\mu dx^\nu$. The holographic principle unifies gravity with the other fundamental forces through the Kaluza-Klein mechanism. The metric for the usual 3+1 extended dimensions of space-time includes the effects of gravity and a cosmological constant, but with six extra compactified dimensions of space also includes the effects of the electromagnetic, strong and weak forces. The action principle follows directly from the geometrical length of the worldline, since the action S is directly proportional to the proper time τ. We understand that the path of least action is like the shortest distance between two points in a curved space-time geometry.

This is where quantum theory enters into the equation. A quantum state of potentiality is a sum over all possible configuration states of information that can become encoded on the observer's holographic screen as the observer follows an accelerated worldline, but the quantum state can also be written as a sum over all possible paths of the observer, and

Chapter 10. Why We Get Sick

each possible path is a possible worldline. The quantum state of potentiality is a sum over all possible worldlines. Quantum theory tells us to weight each possible path with a probability factor that we call the wave function $\psi = e^{i\theta}$, where the phase angle θ is given in terms of the action as $\theta = S/\hbar$, and the action is given in terms of the geometrical length of the worldline. This formulation tells us that the wave function is only a probability factor that arises on the observer's worldline.

The wave-interference nature of this construction insures that the path of least action, which is like the shortest distance between two points in the space-time geometry, will give the maximum quantum probability. In the sense of quantum probability, the configuration states that are most likely perceived by the observer over a sequence of screen outputs are equivalent to the observer following the path of least action, which is like the shortest possible worldline that connects two points in the space-time geometry holographically projected from the screen to the observer. The path of least action is the most likely path in the sense of quantum probability.

There is one big problem with this construction. Quantum theory assumes that the process of quantum state reduction occurs randomly. The quantum state is a sum over all possible configuration states which describes how information can become encoded on the observer's holographic screen in all possible ways. Each quantum state reduction is like a screen output that reduces the quantum state of potentiality of the screen to a particular configuration state of information with each screen output. In the sense of a sum over all possible paths, every screen output is an observational event on the observer's worldline, and every event is a decision point about which path to follow. As long as those decisions are made randomly, in an unbiased way, the path most likely followed in the sense of quantum probability is the path of least action.

What if there is bias in the way the decisions are made? There is nothing in the laws of physics that tells us that the decision making process has to be random or unbiased in nature. The laws of physics, as they determine an action principle only determine a quantum state of potentiality. To state the action S is exactly the same as to state the laws of physics. The quantum state of potentiality is constructed by summing over all possible paths or worldlines of an observer and weighting each path with the probability factor we call the wave function $\psi = e^{i\theta}$, where the phase angle θ is given in terms of the action as $\theta = S/\hbar$. Every observational event on the observer's worldline is a decision point about which path to follow. If these decisions are made randomly, in an unbiased way, then there is predictability in the sense the path of least action is the most likely path. If the decisions are made in a biased way, then all bets are off, and there is no longer any predictability. With biased choice, the laws of physics lose their predictability.

This is a humongous problem in quantum theory that physicists have not been able to solve. First, the decision making process is inherently outside the laws of physics, since those laws can only determine a quantum state of potentiality. An unbiased process of random choice with each quantum state reduction or screen output is hypothesized but there is nothing in the laws of physics that rules out a biased process of choice. A biased decision making process no more violates the laws of physics than a random decision making process. Second, if there is bias in the decision making process, then the laws of physics lose their predictability.

Physicists don't like the possibility of unpredictability and so they have arbitrarily ruled out the possibility of biased choice but there is no good reason in the laws of physics or in quantum theory to do so. Physics really has nothing to say about either the decision making process that reduces the quantum state of potentiality to an actual state or the possibility of biased choice.

It is only this possibility of biased choice, or a biased decision making process, that connects consciousness to physical reality and allows for an understanding of how consciousness can influence the course of physical diseases. More exactly, it is only the focus of attention of consciousness, and the biased choices that arise with the focus of attention that allows us to understand this connection between an observer and the health or illness of an observer's body.

We live in a consensual reality of many different observers. Each observer's world is ultimately limited by its own cosmic horizon, but as the horizons can overlap and become entangled, these different worlds can share information together. The horizon is a bounding surface of space that acts as a holographic screen and encodes information for whatever the observer happens to observe in its own world, but since these worlds are entangled, they share information. In some sense, this is just like an interactive computer network generated virtual reality world displayed on multiple computer screens and observed by multiple observers. Each observer is the consciousness present at the central point of view of its own holographic screen.

Each observer follows a worldline through the space and time holographically projected from its screen to the central point of view of the observer. Every event on that worldline is a decision point about which path to follow. Every event is like a screen output from the observer's screen and with each event the observer faces a choice about which path to follow. The quantum state of potentiality that characterizes the observer's screen is only a sum over all possible paths of the observer, or a sum over all possible configuration states of information that can become encoded on the screen as the observer follows some possible path. At every decision point, the observer faces a choice about which path to follow and which configuration state to observe. If the choices are made in a random or an unbiased way, then the observer will most likely follow the path of least action. If there is bias in the way choices are made, then the observer's path can deviate from the path of least action in unpredictable ways.

The quantum state of potentiality includes information for everything the observer can observe in its world, including its own body. The observable things appear as three

Chapter 10. Why We Get Sick

dimensional objects in space, but all the bits of information are encoded on the observer's holographic screen, including all the information for its own body. The observer's body is only like the central image projected from the screen, like the image of an avatar in a virtual reality world. The observer is looking through the eyes of its avatar, but the avatar is only the central image displayed on the screen, and the observer is the point of consciousness that perceives the screen.

The quantum state of potentiality includes configuration states of information for everything the observer can possibly observe in its world. There is a tendency for bits of information to align together because of quantum entanglement. Entangled bits of information tend to align together over a sequence of events just like entangled spin variables tend to align together. This tendency for bits of information to align together is the very nature of holography which arises from the coherent nature of the wave-interference pattern of the wave function that we see in all quantum phenomena. Alignment of spin variables (as in spin 1 photons) generates the coherent light of a laser, and that coherence leads to the encoding of information on a holographic film in the form of an interference pattern from which the coherent images of a hologram can become projected. In the sense of the holographic principle, we understand that all bound states arise from the tendency of bits of information to align together, like entangled spin variables.

There is also a tendency for the flow of energy through things to come into alignment and for things to follow the path of least action as long as choices are made in an unbiased way. The path of least action is always the most energy efficient path as it expends the least amount of energy like following the shortest distance path between two points. This tendency for bits of information to align together and the flow of energy to come into alignment means that bound states of information tend to form in the observer's world over the course of time.

These bound states of information have a property called coherent organization, which means they tend to self-replicate their forms over a sequence of events. A body is a coherently organized form of information that tends to self-replicate its form over a sequence of events. Such coherently organized forms are included in the quantum state of potentiality that characterizes the observer's world. The quantum state for the observer's world includes all possible ways in which bits of information can become organized into the form of the observer's body which is only the central form of information in the observer's world.

When we speak of the health or disease of the observer's body, we only speak of these possibilities included in the quantum state of potentiality for the observer's world. In order to connect the observer's consciousness, specifically its focus of attention on its world to the possibilities of physical health or disease, we have to address the inherent bias that arises with the focus of attention of the observer's consciousness. This bias of the observer's focus of attention on its world can only arise with the flow of energy through the observer's world.

Chapter 10. Why We Get Sick

If quantum theory turns out to be bogus, as Einstein believed when he stated "God does not play dice", and if physical reality is strictly determined by the laws of physics, then there is no real choice in anything an observer can observe in its world. Everything is strictly determined by the laws of physics. Even if quantum theory does apply, if all choices are made randomly, in an unbiased way, then there also is no real choice, just a roll of the dice. The only way an observer has a real choice about what to observe in its world is if choices are made in a biased way.

There is no denying that each of us has a bias about what we choose to observe in our own world. We express that bias with our focus of attention on things in our world. We are biased to focus our attention on things we like and avoid things we don't like. There is no way to understand the nature of this bias unless there is a biased decision making process.

How does the observer's biased focus of attention on its world arise? What drives this bias in the focus of attention? This is the only entry point that allows us to connect the observer's consciousness to the physical heath or disease of the observer's body.

The only reason this entry point is possible is due to the nature of the quantum state of potentiality that characterizes the observer's world. Every event on the observer's worldline is a decision point where choices are made in terms of which configuration states of information to perceive (as projected from the observer's holographic screen in a screen output) and which path of the observer's worldline to follow. Every event is a decision point where the observer's path branches into all possible paths, and at every decision point the observer faces a choice about which path to follow. The observer can only make these choices as it focuses its attention on the path, and there is inherent bias in the way the choices are made.

What is the nature of this bias? There are two important ways in which the bias can be expressed, but both have to do with the flow of energy. If choices are made in an unbiased way, it is natural for the flow of energy in the observer's world to come into alignment for the reasons discussed above which is the normal way for energy to flow through the observer's world.

When we speak of the flow of energy through the observer's world, we also speak of the flow of energy through the observer's body. The observer's body is a part of its world. The flow of energy through the observer's body animates the observer's body over a sequence of events. The observer's body is only a recognizable form due to the coherent organization of information that allows for the self-replication of form over a sequence of events, but self-replication of form also hinges on the coherent organization of the flow of energy through the observer's body. The observer recognizes this coherent flow of energy through its own body as emotional expressions. These emotional expressions animate the form of the observer's body.

As the flow of emotional energy through the form of the observer's body comes into alignment with the flow of

Chapter 10. Why We Get Sick

energy through other things in the observer's world, feelings of connection are perceived. Feelings of connection feel "good", and so the observer is naturally biased to choose feelings of connection. The observer is biased to choose "good" feelings. As long as the observer chooses feelings of connection, the biased choices the observer makes with its focus of attention on those "good" feelings tend to remain in alignment with the unbiased nature of choice and the normal flow of energy in the observer's world.

As the flow of emotional energy through the form of the observer's body goes out of alignment with the flow of energy through other things in the observer's world, feelings of disconnection are perceived. Feelings of disconnection feel "bad", and so the observer is naturally biased to avoid feelings of disconnection. This bias to avoid "bad" feelings tends to keep the observer's choices in alignment with the unbiased nature of choice and the normal flow of energy.

The observer's bias to choose "good" feelings and avoid "bad" feelings allows for the physical health of the observer's body. This bias tends to keep the observer's choices in alignment with the unbiased nature of choice and the normal flow of energy in the observer's world.

Why would the observer ever choose feelings of disconnection? Why would the observer's focus of attention ever become biased to choose "bad" feelings? The answer has to do with the nature of self-identification and self-defense. Once the observer identifies itself with the form of its body and attributes its existence to arise from its body, it becomes biased to defend the survival of its body as though its existence depends on it. The observer then feels compelled to defend body survival. This feeling is the essence of the fear of non-existence.

Out of this process of self-identification and fear of non-existence, self-defensive expressions arise to defend body survival. These self-defensive expressions are always an interference with the normal flow of energy in the observer's world and lead to feelings of disconnection as the flow of emotional energy through the observer's body goes out of alignment with the normal flow of energy through other things in the observer's world.

Paradoxically, it is these "bad" feelings of disconnection that lead to the disease of the observer's body. Disease arises because the observer chooses to interfere with the normal flow of energy in its world and create a disturbance in the normal flow of energy as the emotional flow of energy through its body goes out of alignment with the normal flow of energy in its world.

The only way physical health is possible is if the flow of energy through the observer's body comes back into alignment, but for that to happen the observer has to detach itself from its world and stop trying to defend the survival of its body as though its existence depends on it. To bring itself back into alignment, the observer has to choose "good" feelings of connection and stop interfering with the normal flow of energy. This is really only possible if the observer stops identifying itself with the form of its body. This

Chapter 10. Why We Get Sick

process of non-identification is only possible if the observer detaches itself from its world. Inherent in the detachment process is the observer's awareness of itself as the consciousness present at the center of its world. Only that presence of consciousness has its own sense of being present, which is its own sense of I-am-ness.

Once the observer attributes its own sense of being present to its body, then the vicious cycle of its self-identification with its body and the self-defense of its body begins. The observer then becomes biased to defend body survival as though its existence depends on it which leads to "bad" feelings of disconnection and the disease of the body. The only way the observer can break this vicious cycle is if the observer detaches itself from its body, stops identifying itself with the form of its body, stops interfering with the normal flow of energy in its world, and stops creating a disturbance in its world with self-defensive expressions.

Once the observer "centers" itself and focuses on its own sense of being present as the consciousness present at the center of its world, the observer then naturally brings itself into alignment with the normal flow of energy in its world and chooses "good" feelings of connection. This is the only decision making process that can lead to the health of the body. This process is confirmed by the Yogic perspective and the Six Sigma methodology.

The one-world-per-observer paradigm and the holographic principle tell us that we truly are "beings of light". These paradigm shattering discoveries tell us that although our bodies are made of physical energy, the true nature of our being is the "light" of consciousness. Just as the images of a physical hologram are illuminated by the physical light of a laser, the images of the physical world we perceive, as projected from a holographic screen to the central point of view of the observer, are illuminated by the "light" of consciousness itself.

10.4 Changes in Atomic Configuration? – An Example

On a recent visit to India, the first author was provided several micron-sized particles that were found at the meditation sites of a physician turned yogi based in Goa, India. A team of his followers inquired if these particles could be analyzed upon his return to Louisville in December. In the initial batch there were six shiny micron-sized particles. With the cooperation of the Director and researchers at the Conn Center for renewable Energy Research, University of Louisville, these particles were analyzed using an optical microscope, a scanning electron microscope, and Raman Spectroscopy. These images are shown in Figures 10.3 – 10.7. On the basis of the analysis, the four particles are: (1) Green Particle – (Cr, Fe) SiO_2, (2) Coral Particle 1 – Copper, (3) Coral Particle 2 – CR_xFeCl6, and (4) Red Particle - $CrAl_2O_4$. The question that remains to be answered is, are these particles an example of meditation changing the atomic configuration of particles that were already at the sites or are such particles of unusual shapes and composition are abundant in nature. Perhaps some readers of this book are crystallographers and might be able to shed light on this topic.

 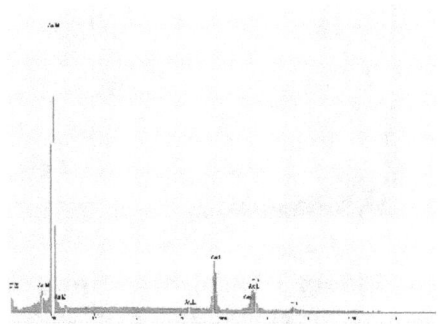

Figure 10.3(a) Image of Particle on SEM Monitor and EDX Spectrum of Particle with Au Line Marked

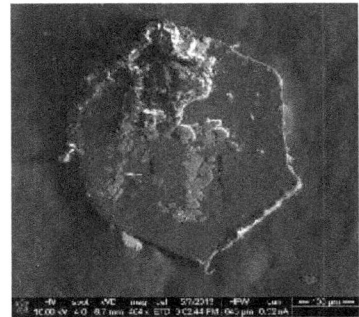 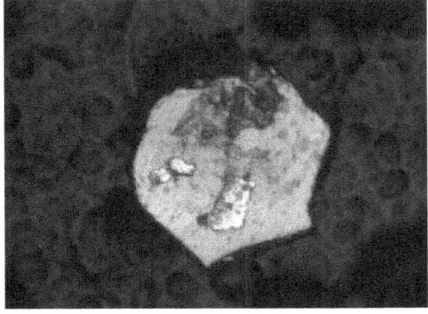

Figure 10.4(a) Image of Green Particle-1 Optical Microscope (Left) and SEM Monitor (Right)

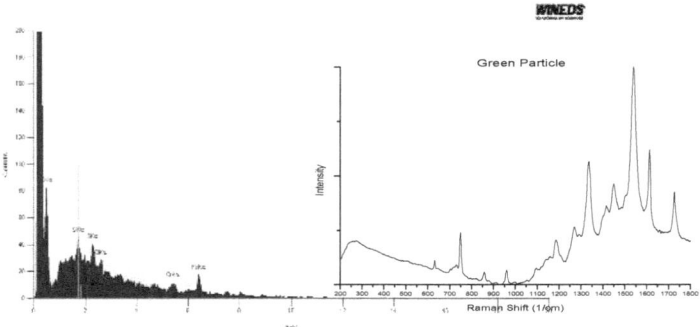

Figure 10.4(b) EDX Spectra of Green Particle-1 (Left) and Raman Spectra (Right)

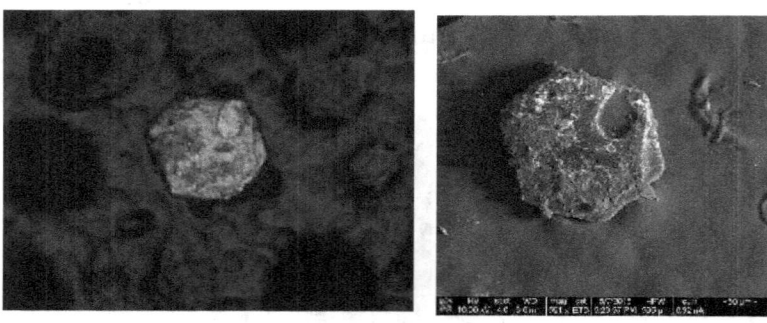

Figure 10.5(a) Image of Coral Particle-1 - Optical Microscope (Left) and SEM Monitor (Right)

Chapter 10. Why We Get Sick

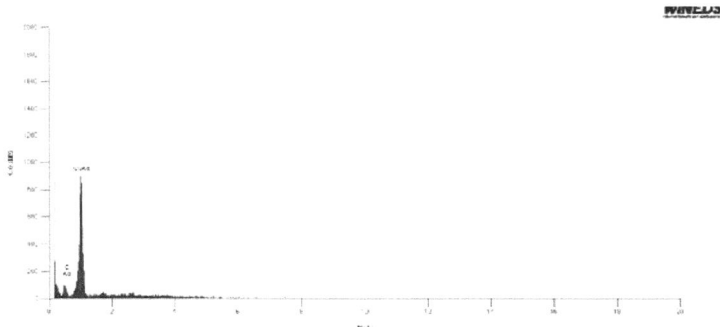

Figure 10.5(b) EDX Spectra of Coral Particle-1: There is no Raman Spectra as the particle is metallic

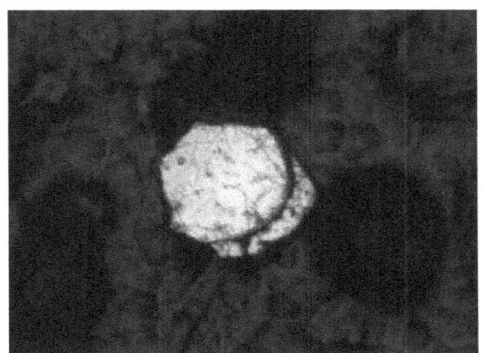

Figure 10.6(a) Image of Coral Particle-2 Optical Microscope (Left): Particle Visible on SEM Monitor but could not capture it as the particle was charging

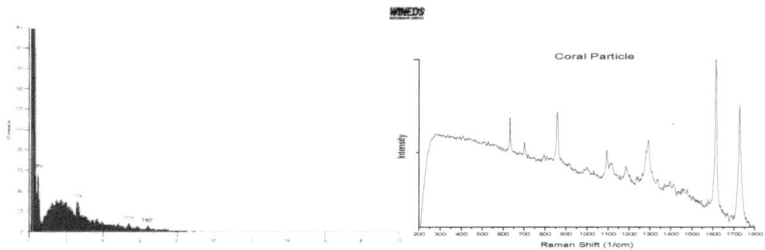

Figure 10.6(b) EDX Spectra of Coral Particle-2 (Left) and Raman Spectra (Right)

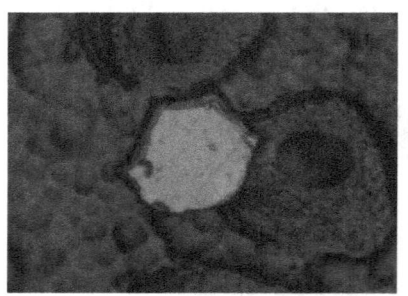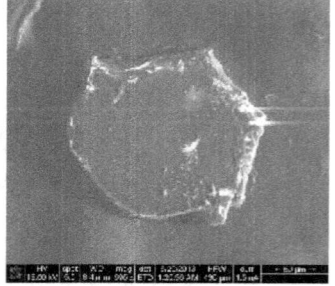

Figure 10.7(a) Image of Red Particle Optical Microscope (Left) and SEM Monitor (Right)

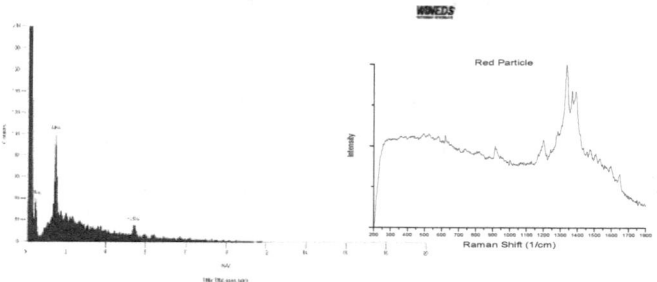

Figure 10.7(b) EDX Spectra of Red Particle (Left) and Raman Spectra (Right)

To Summarize

A yogic and quantum mechanical perspective on why we get sick is presented. According to AMA 80% of illnesses have a psychosomatic component. The yogic perspective presented here posits that 100% of diseases are the product of the mind. In the ensuing chapter we will learn how to get better.

Acknowledgments

The yogic perspectives on diseases is an English translation of the wonderful discourses of Avadhoot Baba Shivanand Ji. The first author is most grateful to Spiritual Science Research Foundation, Goa for the particles found in their meditation halls and to Conn Center for Renewable Energy Research, JB Speed School of Engineering, University of Louisville for help with the analysis of the particles.

Further Reading

[1] Blackburn, Elizabeth and Epel, Elissa, Telomere and Adversity - Too Toxic to Ignore, Nature, 490, 11 October 2012 pp. 169-171.

[2] Deshpande, P. B., Aroskar, S. A., Bhavsar, S. N., and Kulkarni, B. D., Mind Over Matter: Investigation of Materialization of Intentions, Journal of Consciousness Exploration & Research, 5, 2, February 2014.

[3] Deshpande, P. B., Six Sigma for Karma Capitalism, Six Sigma and Advanced Controls, Inc., 2014.

[4] Deshpande, P. B., Sunkara, M., Kulkarni, B. D., Power of Meditation: Materialization of Energy/Intentions, Journal

of Consciousness Exploration and Research, 4. 4, April 2013.

[5] Epel, Elissa, et al., Accelerated Telomere Shortening in Response to Life Stress, Proceedings of the National Academy of Sciences, 101, 49, December 2004. pp. 17312-17315.

[6] Gefter, Amanda, Cosmic Solipsism, (http://fqxi.org/data/essay-contest files/Gefter_Gefter_Fqxi_essay.pdf, 2012).

[7] Harry, J. Mikel and Lawson, J. R., *Six Sigma Productivity Analysis and Process Characterization*, Motorola Press, 1992.

[8] Hawkins, David R., Power vs. Force: Hidden Determinants of Human Behavior, Veritas Publishing, 2004.

[9] Korotkov K.G., Matravers P, Orlov D.V., Williams B.O. Application of Electrophoton Capture (EPC) Analysis Based on Gas Discharge Visualization (GDV) Technique in Medicine: A Systematic Review. The J of Alternative and Complementary Medicine. January 2010, 16, 1, pp.13-25.

[10] Susskind, Leonard, The Black Hole War, Little, Brown and Company, 2008.

CHAPTER 11
How to Raise LOC

A root cause of a problem in life, be it health & wellness, suboptimal performance in any walk of life, and discord and violence is the same; inadequate level of internal excellence or equivalently, inadequate S, R, T level of consciousness. The root cause of that is the weakening of the link of our Atmanic consciousness to the Brahmanic consciousness. Strengthen that link and there will be improvement in all of these things.

In the context of the quest to raise our level of consciousness, level of internal excellence, recall that there are two equivalent representations of the level of consciousness: (1) In terms of S, R, T components, and (2) In terms of positive and negative emotions. For ready reference, positive emotions include such things as unconditional love, empathy, compassion, kindness, etc., while negative emotions include hatred, hostility, anger, fear, anxiety, jealousy, irritation, resentment, despair, etc. There are two approaches to raising our level of consciousness: (1) A conscious approach, and (2) A process whose side-effect is a rise in LOC or equivalently, a rise in positive emotions.

11.1 Conscious Approach

We know that even in the absence of external events our mind thinks of thoughts which in turn can produce emotions. In the previous chapter we saw that positive emotions are life-supporting while negative emotions are life-degrading. So, clearly, we must cultivate positive emotions. The suggested approach is a self-appraisal of negative and positive emotions on a weekly or monthly basis say on a scale of 1 (preponderance of negative emotions) to 5 (preponderance of positive emotions). We need to remember that while external events are not under our control, how we respond to those events is amenable to improvement. And when we say, respond to external events, we mean instantaneous or reflex response, not after we have had time to think how we should respond. The average needs to increase. While the conscious approach appears to be straight forward, it is a necessary but not a sufficient condition for progress. The second approach whose side-effect is a rise in the S component completes the quest for internal excellence.

11.2 Process to raise the S component

This approach is best illustrated with a story, that of the Buddha and the charging elephant. The story involves an external event, namely, sighting of an elephant. The Buddha and his followers were walking in the woods one day when they saw that an elephant was charging at them. Upon seeing this, the followers promptly fled but the Buddha stayed and just raised his hands as though in blessing and the elephant stopped in his track and retreated. To analyze the story in the case of the followers, the external event was sighting of the elephant, their minds perceived the event as a threat, this in turn evoked the emotion of fear, and the action that followed was to flee. The Buddha is an embodiment of positive emotions so when he raised his hands in blessing, these emotions traveled to the elephant's consciousness and the elephant realized no harm was intended and he stopped and retreated.

Two things have to be demonstrated to show that this story is not allegorical; that emotions can travel from human consciousness to the elephant's consciousness and second, the signal can travel sufficiently fast, much faster than the speed of the approaching elephant or else it would be too late.

In chapter 9 we described several scientific experiments showing that emotions can travel over long distances to their own or another person's DNA instantaneously, without a time lag. We also presented two examples, one involving Ellen and her favorite horse Tonopah and the other involving Josh and his favorite dog Mabel showing that the heart rates of the pairs became highly correlated while the respective owner displayed positive emotions when they were with their horse/dog and become uncorrelated when they parted ways.

In a related story, Yoga Guru Paranjothiar relayed the following story to the first author in December 2012. One day, Guruji and two of his followers were driving back from a place called Munnar in Kerala, India, to his Ashram in Thirumoorthi Hills in Tamil Nadu. There was a car in front driving in the same direction when they saw an elephant and her calf on the side of the road who were apparently unperturbed by the cars driving by. Guruji saw that the car in the front stopped and one of the occupants of that car rolled down the window and stuck his hand out with a banana in his hand hoping that the baby elephant would come and take it. Unfortunately, the mother elephant appeared to take this as a threat and began charging at the occupants. Realizing that they were in danger, that car sped away. Now, the mother elephant was alongside Guruji's car with a raised trunk as though ready to attack. Guruji said he raised his hand and the elephant retreated, pretty much like the Buddha's story.

Now the question is how we could move in the direction of the Buddha, i. e., raise our high S component and be endowed with abundant positive emotions. Unlike many other incarnations, we know a lot about the Buddha. We know he was a prince growing up. So, the question is how did he go from being a prince to becoming the Buddha? Although he is known to have been compassionate from childhood, he wouldn't have had the maximum amount of S and minimum amount of R and T needed for enlightenment when was growing up as a prince for if he did, there would have been no further need for enlightenment. There is enough known about him and his works based on which to conclude that he developed the Smax, Rmin, Tmin mindset endowed with abundant positive emotions pursuant to meditation. So, how does meditation achieve the intended result? We now have a considerable explanation.

Chapter 11. How to Raise LOC

As we discussed in the last chapter, 99.9 percent of the body is empty space which houses vibrations and the nature of these vibrations determines the atomic configuration and therefore cellular structure which in turn determines whether we are well or unwell. If the frequency of these vibrations is not life-supporting all the undesirable effects follow. The source of these vibrations is the past psychic impressions. If the psychic impressions are life supporting (positive emotions), then life-giving changes occur in the cells but if they are life-degrading (negative emotions), then cellular changes too are life-degrading. What meditation does is to wipe out the past negative psychic impressions. And how do we know this hypothesis has merit? Meditation will experientially convince the practitioner of an enhanced capacity to remain centered in the presence of severe external conditions, something he/she did not possess short time ago. Furthermore, there will be numerous medical tell-tale signs.

11.3 Evidence

Appendix 1 lists many publications on the benefits of meditation in variety of areas of life in top class journals, not just health. The appendix also lists numerous CEOs and four Nobel Laureates who are regular meditators. There are many fine examples of the beneficial effects of meditation. One is a successful application of meditation in prisons. Figure 11.1 (a) – (c) depict the bioenergy measurements of a man named Alfonso at the start and at the end of a mediation program. The starting bioenergy field is disrupted, stress level is on the high side of normal and the chakras are too small (low

134 | *Chapter 11. How to Raise LOC*

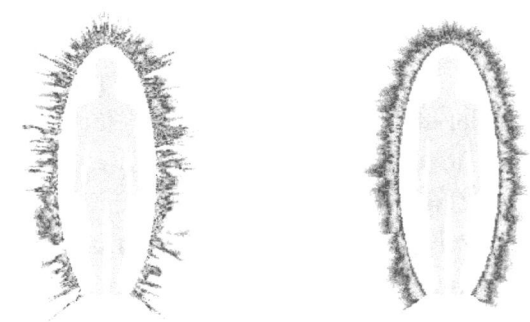

Figure 11.1 (a) Bioenergy Field

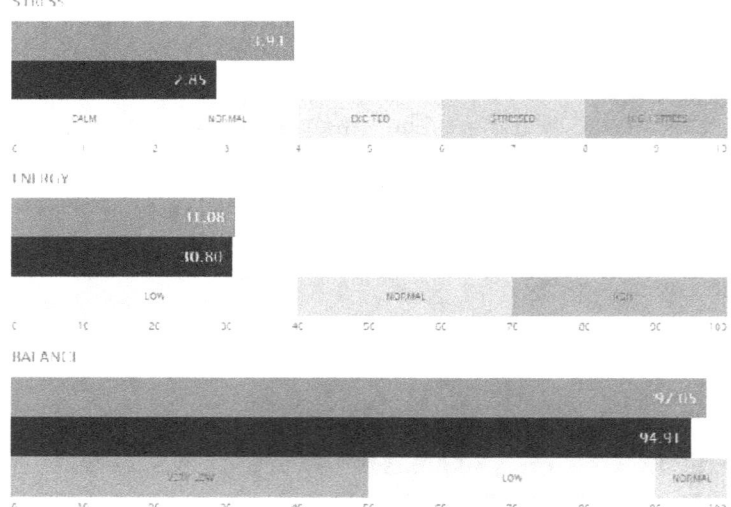

Figure 11.1 (b) Stress, Energy, Balance

energy). The improvement is obvious. The chakras are still too small but better aligned. The aspirant understood the warning signs, made life-style choices, and added meditation to his daily routine.

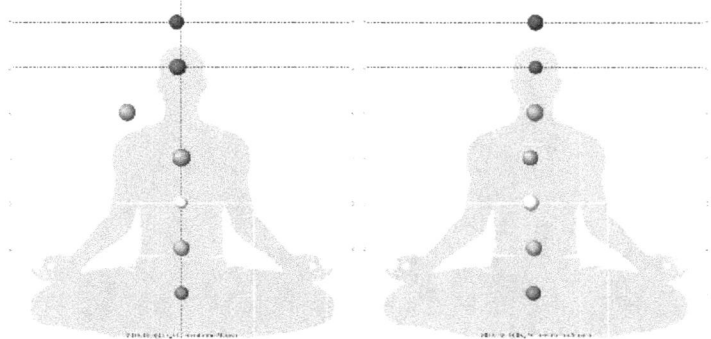

Figure 11.1 (c) Chakras

Figure 11.1 Bioenergy Measurements of Alfonso Before and After Meditation

Scientists Matthieu Ricard, PhD (Pasteur Institute, Paris) and R. J. Davidson, PhD (Harvard) and associates have studied the brainwave changes of experienced meditators occurring during mindfulness meditation practice and compared the results with controls who had no meditation experience. They found very significant differences (Lutz, et al., 2004). Davidson is an endowed Professor of Psychology and Psychiatry at the University of Wisconsin. Ricard obtained his doctorate in Genetics under Nobel Laureate Prof. Laureate Francois Jacob. Ricard is a recipient of the French Order of Merit and he accompanies HH Dalai Lama as an interpreter whenever HHDL travels to France. Ricard lives in the Himalayas.

Figure 11.2 depicts the bioenergy measurements of Guru Mahan Maharishi Paranjothiar measurements on May 26, 2013. So, by now we have seen the GDV diagrams of a healthy individual in chapter 8, one who is quite unwell in

136 | Chapter 11. How to Raise LOC

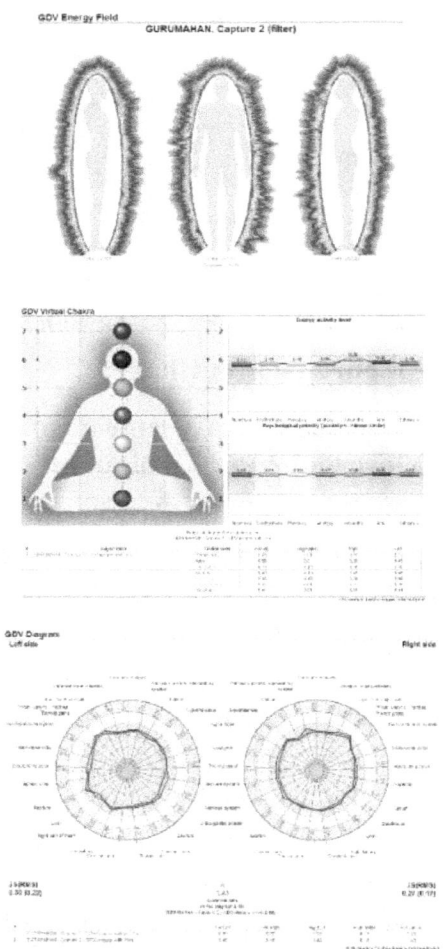

Figure 11.2 Bioenergy Measurements of Guru Mahan Maharishi Paranjothiar

chapter 10, and now a self-realized yogi with at a high level of consciousness. In the following two chapters we present a more detailed wherewithal of how to progress in our quest to raise LOC.

Chapter 11. How to Raise LOC

Nobel Laureate Elizabeth Blackburn and colleague Elissa Epel have shown that meditation has a restorative effect on telomere length. The investigators also found that while exercises, eating healthy, social support, etc., were all restorative, meditation was the most effective intervention capable of slowing the erosion of telomeres. That prompted cnn.com to publish a column in July 2014 headlined, *Can Meditation Really Reverse Aging?* Her work also earned her the title of Medicine Buddha from fellow Nobel Laureate HH Dalai Lama.

Prachi Verma penned a column in the Economic Times, titled *Maruti Staffers Tank Up on Spiritual Wisdom* (12 September 2014) in which she described how the Indian automobile company was benefitting from programs on internal excellence. Earlier, Manager Atul Jain could not tolerate a Single glitch in the processes handled by his team and this led to frequent unpleasant situations. As a result, many of his subordinates hesitated to acknowledge their gaffes. Now, the picture has changed and Jain's team finds itself more in harmony than ever before. She quotes Jain as saying, *After attending these in-house sessions, my efficiency as well as that of my department has risen. The ownership in my team members has also improved. They no longer hesitate in disclosing their mistakes.* Encouraged by the response, the company which had been struggling to handle workplace conflicts, introduced sessions on spirituality by the Brahmakumaris for all its 18,000 employees. Says the column, Celebrity Brahmakumari Shivani will conduct the sessions on spiritual well-being. The sessions will help employees keep stress levels in control, keep emotions in check, and avoid conflicts. In this context, in a later chapter we show that in the absence of internal excellence, six sigma programs deliver suboptimal performance. The case-study at Maruti Suzuki is an example of the case in point.

11.4 The Roots of Meditation

YODA (YOga + VeDA) of the Star Wars fame really is the origin of meditation. Yoga literally means *To Connect*. But connect what with what? The answer, connect Brahmanic consciousness to the Atmanic consciousness. The real power of yoga is materialization of intentions with meditation, the subject of an ensuing chapter, but to the yogi the sole intention worthy of materialization is to be ever in *Turya Avastha*, to be in the Anandmaya Kosha, always connected to Brahmanic consciousness, always blissful unaffected by highly unfavorable and excitingly pleasant conditions that are part and parcel of life. Meditation is an important part of Patanjali's (~500 bce) eight-fold yoga system. Success with meditation is enhanced by the wellness of external systems and internal organs and systems. Add ethical living and proper diet to the list and it is a complete recipe not just for wellness but also for transformation. The following are parts of Patanjali's yoga system related to diet and external and internal systems:

1. **The Food We Eat.** The food we consume is the first source of variability in health and wellness. Of course, we have the traditional dietary guidelines from FDA but for progress in the present context, yogis suggest we limit our food intake primary to Positive Pranic Foods:

Vegetarian food with limited spices, lentils, wheat, rice, etc. (A taste of Isha: Recipe for the Pranic Life Style, A Publication of the Isha Yoga Foundation, undated).
2. **External Subsystem.** Yogasanas or other forms of physical exercises that target the various elements of the external subsystem including joints, spine, and muscles is a way forward to restoring/maintaining the wellbeing of the external subsystem.
3. **Internal Organs and Subsystem.** The Pranayam breathing exercises, the topic of the next chapter, maximize the capture of bioenergy from the cosmos and restore the internal organs and subsystems to their normal state.

Further Reading

[1] Blackburn, Elizabeth and Epel, Elissa, Telomere and Adversity - Too Toxic to Ignore, Nature, 490, 11 October 2012 pp. 169-171.

[2] Chez, Ronald, A., Ed., Proceedings: Measuring the Human Energy Field – State of the Science, The Gerontology Research Center, National Institute on Aging, National Institute of Health, Baltimore, MD April 17 - 18, 2002.

[3] Deshpande, P. B. and Kowall, J. P., Yogic Perspective on Health, Six Sigma Assessment, and Quantum Physics Approach, Journal of Consciousness Exploration & Research, 5, 3, April 2014.

[4] Epel, Elissa, et al., Accelerated Telomere Shortening in Response to Life Stress, Proceedings of the National

Academy of Sciences, 101, 49, December 2004. pp. 17312-17315.

[5] Lutz, Antoine, et al., Long-Term Meditators Self-induce High Amplitude Gamma-Wave Synchrony During Mental Practice, Proc. Nat. Acad. Sciences, 101 (46) Nov. 6, 2004.

[6] Marchant, Jo, Can Meditation Really Slow Aging, www.cnn.com, Jul 10, 2014.

[7] Verma, Prachi, Maruti Staffers Tank up on Spiritual Wisdom, The Economic Times, September 12, 2014.

[8] www.davidlynchfoundation.org/prisons.html

CHAPTER 12
Pranayam

Pranayam or *Control of Prana* refers to control of pranic energy. In practical terms, it may be interpreted as a set of breathing exercises which maximize the life-force - Pranic Energy - and oxygen intake. As already mentioned the human system consists of five sheaths the second of which is the Pranamaya Kosha or Pranic sheath. Yogis say that we can receive 20% of our energy needs from the cosmos via breathing provided correct practices are adopted. Pranayam facilitates this Pranic energy maximization and delivers numerous health and wellness benefits. These ancient Indian breathing exercises are effective for a variety of ailments. The first author has been doing them for a decade and has experienced a number of benefits including relief of constipation, hyper acidity, and nasal allergies. This chapter is inspired by the work of Swami Ramdev of Hardwar, India who demonstrates how these exercises are done in a DVD produced by the Divya Yoga Trust (http://www.divyayoga.com). In this chapter we discuss Pranayam and present a case study illustrative of its health benefits. The material in the chapter is meant to be of instructional nature. Before undertaking any of these exercises, interested readers must secure their doctor's permission and learn how to do the exercises properly from a qualified professional who will likely have you (and your heirs) sign a liability waiver as is customary with any exercise program. To assess if it is safe for you to do these exercises, your doctor may wish to see how these exercises are done and Swami Ramdev's DVD on Pranayam may serve this purpose as well.

12.1 Swami Ramdev's Pranayam Program

These exercises are to be done on an empty stomach, four to five hours after a meal and so mornings appear to be the best time for them. The sitting posture for these exercises is comfortable sitting position on a floor-mat or chair with spine, shoulders, neck, and head held upright. Breathing should be from the chest as the organs responsible for breathing are the lungs. The Pranayam program consists of eight exercises:

1. Omkar (Warm-up Pranayam). Inhale deeply and as you exhale, chant Aum for the duration of the exhalation process. Do this eleven times. Ancient works all give importance to Aum signifying the beginning of all creation.

2. Bhastrika (Inhale-Exhale) Pranayam. This exercise involves noiseless deep inhalation and exhalation for five minutes. The duration of inhalation and exhalation should be roughly the same. This exercise appears to work on the nasal system and sinuses. Also, this and most other exercises appear to work on the lungs.

3. Kapalbhati (Exhale-Exhale) Pranayam. Much importance is given to this Pranayam. RgVed is where it is first referenced. In this Pranayam, focus on exhale alone for fifteen minutes. Suck your stomach in at each exhalation but inhalation is passive and automatic. The mechanics of Kapalbhati makes the stomach go in and out. This exercise appears to work on several organs including the kidneys, intestine, colon, pancreas, liver, etc., potentially impacting on intra-abdominal fat which physicians say is a biomarker for heart attacks.

4. Bahya (Suck-in Stomach) Pranayam. In this Pranayam take a deep breath and forcefully exhale. When the exhalation is complete drop your chin down so no air can enter the system. Now, suck the stomach in, lift the abdomen up, and hold in this position for fifteen seconds. Then left your chin, relax the abdomen, return the stomach to its normal position, and inhale. This exercise is be done three to five times. This exercise appears to work on the bladder, reproductive system, urinary system, and the colon.

5. Anulom-Vilom (Alternate Nostril) Pranayam. This Pranayam involves breathing through alternate nostrils. Close your right nostril with your right thumb and take a deep breath but noiselessly from the left nostril. Once inhalation is complete, close your left nostril with the middle and third fingers of your right hand and exhale from your right nostril. Once exhalation is complete, inhale from the right nostril while holding the left nostril closed. Once inhalation is complete, close your right nostril with your right thumb and exhale from the left nostril. This constitutes one cycle. This exercise is to be done for fifteen minutes. Here, the duration of inhalation and exhalation should be roughly the same. The most direct impact of this exercise appears to be on the nasal systems and sinuses but Swami

Ramdev suggests it provides several other benefits such as purification of nerves, effect on arteries, etc.

6. Ujjayi (Constrict Throat) Pranayam. To do this exercise, constrict your throat as you inhale so a somewhat peculiar sound is heard. When inhalation is complete, drop your chin down so your breath remains arrested. Hold to the count of 15 seconds and then lift your chin, place your right thumb on your right nostril, and let all the air out of the left nostril. This is one cycle. This exercise is be done five times. This exercise may be seen to be impacting on the throat and is suggested to reduce snoring and have a positive impact on thyroid and throat problems.

7. Bhramari (Bumblebee) Pranayam. To do this Pranayam, block out external sounds by placing your thumbs on the respective ears (Tragus), your forefingers on the forehead, and your middle fingers on the spot between your eyes and the bridge of your nose (Canthus), and the little finger and the third finger close to the middle finger. With this posture established, inhale deeply and with exhalation make the sound of the bee. This exercise is to be done five times. This exercise is said to be beneficial for headaches.

8. Omkar (Cool-down) Pranayam. This Pranayam is the same as the first. Do it ten times.

12.2 How Pranayam Improves Health

Pranayam improves health in several ways:

1. At the physical level, Pranayam is one of the few methods available for exercising internal organs and systems, from nasal systems and sinuses all the way to urinary and GI tracts. Combining exercises for external systems

(muscles, joints, etc.) such as Asanas, workouts at a Gym, swimming, walking, etc., together with Pranayam exercises for internal organs and systems appears to make perfect sense. Secondly, Pranayam maximizes our energy capture. In a few weeks of regular practice, the aspirant will begin to realize this experientially.

2. The genius of Patanjali, credited with introducing Pranayam about 500 bce, has been endorsed by enlightened individuals such as the late Swami Vivekananda, Yoga Guru the late B. K. S. Iyengar and scores of yogis. Swami Ramdev has popularized Pranayam among hundreds of million in India.

12.3 Case Study – Louisville Pranayam Group

A group of nineteen Louisville area friends volunteered for the study in the fall of 2005. The group included medical doctors, professors, senior engineering personnel, home makers, etc. The author provided each participant with a DVD on Pranayam marketed by Divya Yoga Trust and trained them in the exercises. They were also given an overview of six sigma. They then practiced Pranayam for three months to assess the health benefits. The selected quantitative health parameters were measured in a pathology laboratory, courtesy of Dr. Rajan Amin, MD in Louisville. Each measurement was made twice to ascertain repeatability and reproducibility. Participants were asked to rate qualitative parameters on a scale of 1 (problem nonexistent) to 5 (problem acute or chronic). At the end of the program each participant provided a short paragraph on his or her experience with Pranayam. In the narrative, participants primarily focused on those qualitative variables pertinent to them.

Eighteen out of nineteen participants reported a sense of calm, higher energy levels, and increased stamina. Even the nineteenth participant, who didn't feel any difference, has been hooked on these exercises and does them regularly. Participants who had issues with sleep, control over bowel movement, constipation, hyperacidity, and snoring reported substantial improvement. Cholesterol and fasting sugar levels of a couple of participants came down from higher than the upper limit of normal to lower than the same limit. Cholesterol and fasting sugar level benefit for participants whose values were not far away from the normal range was minimal. Generally, laboratory results indicated that not all individuals benefited to the same extent. This is to be expected given the nonlinear nature of human systems. Some benefits may accrue early in the program while some may take longer. Very significant benefits may be accruing but the evidence may come only sometime later, may be years later, for example involving the cardio reactive protein as pointed out by participant, Dr. Kailash Sabharwal, an endocrinologist in the group. Now, that a device is available to measure our bioenergy (GDV), it is possible to assess the efficacy of Pranayam as a means to increase the energy.

References

[1] **Deshpande, P. B.**, A Small Step for Man: Zero to Infinity with Six Sigma, Six Sigma and Advanced Controls, Inc., Louisville, KY 2009.

[2] **Govindan, M.**, *Babaji and the eighteen Siddha Kriya Yoga Tradition*, Babaji Kriya Yoga Order of Acharyas Trust Bangalore, India, 2004.

[3] **Iyengar, B. K. S.**, *Light on Pranayama*, Harper Collins Publishers, India 2008.

[4] **Swami Vivekananda**, Raj Yoga, Ramkrishna Math, Math, Nagpur India 1961.

CHAPTER 13
Meditation for Materialization of Intentions

Amanda Gefter showed how something, the universe, came out of nothing which she called the void. Jim Kowall showed that the nothingness of the void cannot be anything else but (Brahmanic) consciousness. The results of several scientific experiments revealed that Atmanic consciousness is a microcosm of Brahmanic consciousness and that the two remain connected forever. Since Brahmanic consciousness has created the universe from nothing and since our consciousness is a microcosm of Brahmanic consciousness, it just may be that we too can create, i. e., materialize our intentions. This may well be the basis for the ancient verse *Aham Brahmasmi* (*I am the Creator*). We have also explained that to reach the Atmanic consciousness it is essential to increase our level of consciousness and to do that it is necessary to remove the obstacles to progress.

In Chapter 10 we explained that meditation was a key to raising the level of consciousness, level of internal excellence. It was also pointed out that meditation had the capacity to materialize intentions but that to the yogi the only intention worthy of materialization was to always be in the *Turya Avastha*, always connected to the Brahmanic consciousness. However for the rest of us, the pursuit can bring material benefits including health and wellness, exemplary performance in all walks of life, less discord and violence. Chapter 10 presented several examples illustrative of the benefits of meditation. In this chapter we present a formal program for materialization of intentions. The program is amenable to six sigma assessment but it is not quite science because of repeatability and reproducibility issues.

The Late Maharishi Mahesh Yogi had the vision of transforming this into a more peaceful world. Materialization of intentions was a key element of that vision. The six yogis to whom this book is dedicated are continuing that quest. Numerous scientists investigating Maharishi's program over several decades had found it to be credible. Numerous scientific papers on his program have appeared in reputed international journals.

In the Aristotle era (Born 384 BCE) lasting some two thousand years, it was widely believed that the planet Earth was at the center of our solar system. That began to change when Copernicus discovered in the 15th Century that the Sun was at the center. Galileo was put under house arrest in the 16th Century for subscribing to the Copernican model. The widespread acceptance of the heliocentric model of the solar system ushered in the first Copernican revolution of thought. That revolution enabled tremendous strides in science over the course of the ensuing five hundred years or so to the present time. However, throughout this period, mainstream scientists have steadfastly maintained that consciousness, intentions, and emotions cannot possibly influence physical reality. This situation is slowly changing

Chapter 13. Meditation for Materialization of Intentions

judging by the high quality publications and scores of well-known personalities subscribing to meditation practice. To understand this further, consider Equation (13.1) we refer as the Tiller hypothesis:

$$Q_T = Q_{P1} + \alpha Q_{P2} \qquad (13.1)$$

W. A. "Bill" Tiller is an eminent Professor Emeritus and former Chair of the Department of Materials Science and Engineering at Stanford University. In Equation (13.1) Q_T is the total measurement, Q_{p1} is the current reality, α is an activity coefficient ($0 \leq \alpha \leq 1$), and Q_{p2} is the psycho-energetic component. Ordinarily $\alpha = 0$ and therefore the total measurement is reflective of the current reality. However, when α becomes nonzero, the total measurement will reflect the intended, new reality. In the light of the Brahma Uncertainty Principle, a slight modification to Equation (13.1) is proposed:

$$Q_T = Q_{P1} + \alpha(LOC)Q_{P2} \qquad (13.2)$$

Where $\alpha(LOC)$ is a parameter associated with the level of consciousness. Tiller realizes the functional dependence but it may be better to state it explicitly. Materialization of intentions may be seen as the pursuit to render α nonzero. Tiller has shown that an intention can not only be materialized but it can also be imprinted on an electrical device he calls Intention Electrical Device (IED) for use elsewhere (www.tiller.org). The intention is imprinted on the device by a meditative practice which included Coherence + Intention. As an example, Tiller has presented a case study involving the raising or lowering the pH of water by 1 unit without the addition of any chemicals. Figure

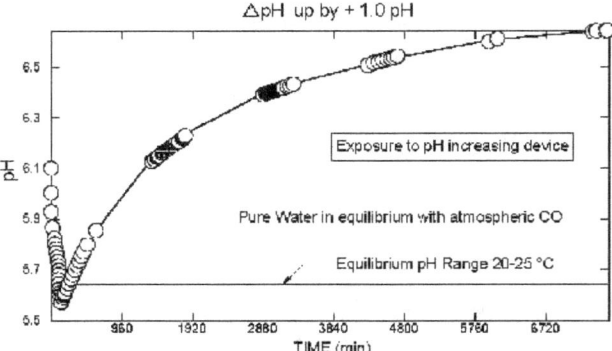

Figure 13.1 Raising the pH of Water by one unit by Intention Alone (www.tiller.org).

13.1 is a plot from their study for the intention of increasing the pH by 1 unit. The pH of water is seen to decrease initially as the water equilibrates with the surrounding air and then rises over time to reach the intended +1 unit change in pH. The accuracy of the pH system is reported to be ± 0.02. According to Tiller, these results have been reproduced at ten different laboratories in the US and Europe but the IED was always imprinted at their home-base in Arizona for use in these ten laboratories.

The extent to which the new reality materializes increases with increasing values of α. Now, if multiple experiments were conducted to test the Tiller hypothesis, several will likely fail and herein lies a problem for science. Science demands that for a hypothesis to be acceptable, it must be possible to repeat an experiment and obtain the same results regardless of who conducts the experiment, how many times, and where, and that is the way it should be. The problem is not with the Tiller hypothesis or science but that the activity coefficient is a function of the level of consciousness of the tester among other unknown and uncontrollable causes. We have coined the name Brahma Uncertainty Principle for this type of uncertainty (Deshpande and Kulkarni, 2012). Thus, science is not the proper framework to examine the Tiller hypothesis, six sigma is.

Six Sigma is a fundamental methodology for problem solving that is based solely on input-output data. Such approaches are called systemic approaches to problem solving. Fundamental, mechanistic approaches to problem-solving should always be preferred but when sufficiently-detailed knowledge of the system under scrutiny is unavailable, six sigma is the appropriate tool to use. Such is the case with human beings. We all are multivariable, nonlinear, self-regulating, and evolving as we age. Unlike science which demands that the results of every experiment be repeatable and reproducible, six sigma posits that there will always be a certain amount of inherent and inevitable variation in the outcomes due to uncontrollable and unknown causes.

Statisticians refer to these factors as common causes. In human beings, the common cause variability arises for two reasons: One source is what we inherit from our ancestors (*Sanchet Karma*) and the other is what we accumulate by our own actions from the time of birth to the present age (*Prarabddha Karma*). These lead to psychic impressions in the fourth energy sheath we have discussed earlier. Thus, common cause variability precludes zero defects ad infinitum. That is, if a sufficiently large random sample of aspirants were to undertake the program of materialization on intentions, no matter how well it is designed, understood, and practiced, not all will succeed. The goal of six sigma is to uncover all discoverable sources of variation so that maximum number of aspirants will achieve their goal.

Chemical engineers might wonder if the change in the hydrogen and hydroxyl ion concentration reported in the Tiller experiment violates the conservation of mass principle since no chemicals were added. In the example soon to be presented involving meditators lifting off the ground we encountered a similar dilemma. Were the meditators defying the Newton's Law of Gravity? Our current understanding of the laws of nature is that they can never be violated although in some cases we may not fully comprehend them. However, intentions may manipulate the system and deliver the intended results without ever violating the fundamental laws of nature. Thus, in the context of the Tiller example, it is possible that the intention has caused the output of the pH measuring system to undergo the desired change but the pH of water itself has not changed. Similarly, in the levitation example, meditators have made themselves sufficiently light to lift off the ground and not that they have remained heavy and still lifted off the ground.

The example of the Institute of HeartMath in Chapter 9 is an excellent illustration of the case in point. They showed that with heart coherence + intention, meditators could wind or unwind a strand of DNA in a beaker located several feet away. Coherence has a bearing on positive emotions and therefore, level of consciousness. Without coherence, intentions have no prospects of materialization. IHM markets a coherence increasing device called *Inner Balance* which works with a smart phone App that is easy to use.

Chapter 13. Meditation for Materialization of Intentions

We were also inspired by the daily discourses of Baba Shivanand Ji (www.shivyog.com) in India on Z-TV where he regularly speaks of the wherewithal for the materialization of intentions using Durga Saptashati – 700 shlokas of Durga. To continue, Larry King asked the Late Maharishi Mahesh Yogi in a CNN TV interview on May 12, 2002, what is transcendental meditation? Maharishi replied:

> *Transcendental meditation is a means to do what one wants to do in a better way, in the right way for maximum results. It's a program in which the mind begins to experience its own finer impressions, finer thoughts, and then finally transcends the finest thought to the level called self-referral consciousness, the ultimate reality of life. This is pure intelligence from where the creation emerges, from where the administration of life is maintained, and from where the physical expression of the universe has its basis. Transcendental meditation brings about transcendental consciousness, which is self-referral consciousness, the source of all intelligence.*

Later in the interview, Larry asked, What is Yogic Flying? Maharishi responded:

> *It is that level of creative intelligence in the self-referral consciousness that will materialize the intentions. Whatever the intentions, materialize the intentions.*

Larry King appeared to remain puzzled throughout the interview. The interview is available on YouTube at (http://www.youtube.com/watch?v=0icNZnUxYo0&feature=relmfu). The reader is also encouraged to view a video at http://www.youtube.com/watch?v=k1cwMc4Myvg.

13.1 Six Sigma Project for Materialization of Intentions

Here, we present the contours of a six sigma project for the materialization of intentions. We have coined the name *Sankalpa Siddhi Sadhana* for the program. In Sanskrit, Sankalpa means intention(s), siddhi means realization, and Sadhana means meditation. The name resonated with us as the scientific framework for external excellence, six sigma, also has *s* as the first letter in each of the two words. Thus, the 2s's for external excellence plus the 3s's for internal excellence equates to 5s's for wholesome excellence.

Central Premise: An intention imprinted in the deepest recesses of our consciousness materializes. Negative psychic impressions are obstacles to progress and must be eliminated to realize the goal.

Program Objective: Design, implement, and assess the performance of a process for testing the hypothesis of materialization of intentions with six sigma principles.

Outcomes: The outcome measures (intentions) of general interest are improvement in health & wellbeing, interpersonal relations, exemplary performance in all aspects of life including business and academic performance, enhanced creativity and innovativeness, less discord, better decision making.

Tools for investigating the hypothesis: The principal tools available are: (i) *Meditation practices as gleaned from the*

Sanskrit Yoga Sutras of Patanjali and Tamil Tirumantiram of Tirumular (Govindan, 2003) and (ii) what at first glance may deceptively appear as religious practices in Durga Saptashati program of Baba Shivanand Ji. In our line of thinking, there is really no difference between these approaches. We may use whichever resonates with us. The parameters to be optimized are: (1) Stepwise process, (2) Chronology, and (3) Duration.

We all remain connected to the cosmic consciousness at some level with an invisible field of energy just as everything was at the time of the Big Bang. This energy field has enormous intelligence in that it responds to the power of human emotions. Therefore, we may tap into this field using emotions as the language of communication. Even temporary access to this field will bring enormous benefits. Connecting to the "Net" is important if our pursuit of materializing intentions is to succeed.

A topic related to connecting to the Net is the notion of *Purusha* and *Prakrati* of the Samkhya philosophy. Patanjali begins with the verse, *Atha Yoganushasanam* (I am exposing you henceforth to the science of Yoga). Patanjali appears to assume that the reader is familiar with the concept of Purusha and Prakrati. To briefly explain, there are two basic principles from which the universe is deemed to have manifested. *Purusha* - characterized by cosmic consciousness through which he, Purusha, observes, witnesses, and supervises *Prakrati*. At the cosmic level, whatever has been created is nothing but Prakrati. At the level of a living being, there is also a *purusha* and *Prakrati* which are microcosmic parts of the cosmic Purusha and cosmic Prakrati, respectively. Without purusha, Prakrati can do nothing. Our Prakrati includes the five senses, five sense organs, five sense faculties, five energy sheaths, and five different types of sense objects (panch mahaboot - five creative elements - Earth/matter, water/liquid, fire/heat, air, and Ether/space).

Purusha (cosmic consciousness) is ever present, unchanging, above and beyond the pairs of opposites (e. g., happiness/sorrow; love/hate, etc.) and defects of any kind. Individual purusha being a microcosm of the cosmic Purusha, the potential for purusha to acquire the attributes of Purusha exist. The obstacles to progress are the negative psychic impressions in the fourth energy sheath, Dnyanamaya Kosha. Because of this, they control our Prakrati rather than our purusha. The meditative practices are *intended* to remove this obstacle. When this obstacle is removed, the individual consciousness gets connected to the cosmic consciousness. Patanjali's Yoga Sutras (Vedic Sanskrit tradition) and Tirumular's Tirumantiram (Ancient Tamil tradition) suggest that meditating on a specific sutra will materialize the associated intentions (see e.g., sutra 4.1). It may therefore be reasonable to include in our practices the intention of removing the obstacles and endowing us with the understanding of Purusha and Prakrati. Prakrati cannot exist without Purusha and therefore the intention must include both. Connection to the Net is synonymous to connecting our consciousness with the cosmic consciousness.

Having opted for the Yoga Sutras to investigate the phenomenon of materialization of intentions, there is an immediate problem. There are 195 sutras - aphorisms - (In the case of Durga Saptashati there are 700 verses). The question is how many of them should be included in the meditative practices and which ones. Each of them has associated with it one or more specific thought/intention/emotion and therefore, the selection of the correct ones could conceivably spell the difference between success and failure. The chronology and duration too are likely to be major impact factors. We have selected some twenty sutras for this six sigma project. We leave it to the readers to select their own set of sutras and carry out the investigation and evaluate the efficacy of their selection. We site several sutras taken from Govindan (2003) for illustrative purposes:

13.2 Select Yoga Sutras

A sutra on Purusha and Prakrati is:

Sva-svami-saktyoh sva-rupa-upalabdhi-hetuh samyogah

2.33

The union (coming together) of the owner (purusha) and the owned (prakriti) leads to the recognition of the essence and power of them both.

In sutra 2.17, Patanjali says, the reason for suffering is that we confuse the Seer (purusha) with the Seen, the constituent forces of nature (Prakrati), and this suffering leads to fluctuations of our consciousness which is an obstacle to progress.

A couple of sutras outlining the obstacles to progress are:

Chapter 13. Meditation for Materialization of Intentions

Vyadhi-styana-samasya-pramada-alasya-avirati-bhranti-darsana-bhumikatva-anavasthitvatvani citta-viksepas-te'ntarayah

Translation:

Disease, dullness, doubt, carelessness, lethargy, absence of detachment, false perception, inability to reach firm ground, and instability cause fluctuations of consciousness and become obstacles.

And

Drg-darsana-saktyor-eka-atmata-iva-asmita **2.6**

Personal ego identifies the power of the Seer (Purusha) with that of the instrument of Seeing (body-mind).

Sutras 1.32 and 2.11 provide the path forward for progress.

Tat-pratisedha-artham-eka-tatva-abhyasah **1.32**

Translation:

The practice of concentration on a single object is the best way to overcome the obstacles.

And

Dhyana-heyas-tad-vritayah **2.11**

Translation:

These fluctuations of our consciousness are discarded by meditation.

By now in the book a strong link has been established between positive emotions (unconditional love, compassion, kindness, empathy, etc.), reduced fluctuations in and rising levels of consciousness, internal excellence, health & wellness, and exemplary business performance. So you may wish to include them in your meditative practices. Patanjali narrates the path forward for progress:

> *Maitry-adisu balani* (3.23)

By communion [samyama: Dharana (concentration), Dhyana (meditation), Samadhi (contemplation)] on friendliness and other such qualities, the power to transmit them is attained.

There are other sutras related to positive emotions; one is:

> *Vitarka-badhane pratipaksa-bhavanam* (2.33)

Translation:

When bound by negative thoughts, their opposites (positive ones) should be cultivated. This is pratipaksha bhavanam.

The importance of cultivating positive emotions is further explained in the next sutra:

> *Vitarka: himsa-adayah krta-karita-anumodita lobha-krodha-moha-purvaka*
>
> *Mrdu-madhya-ahimatra dukha-ajnana-ananta-phalaiti pratipaksha-bhavanam*

Translation:

Negative thoughts or acts such as violence, etc., done by us or by someone else on our behalf, or endorsed by us, whether incited by greed, anger, or infatuation, whether indulged in with mild, moderate, or strong intentions result in endless ignorance and unhappiness. Hence, the need for the cultivation of opposite thoughts (pratipaksha bhavanam).

Now, materialization of intentions giving the desired outcomes could take time measured in months or even years. Levitation may serve as a valuable intermediate observation indicative of progress with our meditative practices. This is important because in the absence of an intermediate result, we may discover too late why we did not succeed. It is important to remember that levitation happens; we do not try to levitate. Patanjali's yoga sutras related to levitation are 3.39 and 3.42: The sutra 3.42 is:

kaya-akasayo Sambandha-samyamat laghu-talasampatteh ca akasa-gamanam
Translation:

When we concentrate (sanyama) upon the gap between the skin of our body and the adjoining space, lightness of objects such as cotton and the capacity to travel across space are acquired.

In an earlier publication Deshpande, et al., (2011) outlined a scientific explanation of levitation during meditation using principles of fluidization widely known in chemical engineering. The practices render an aspirant light as cotton and so he lifts up from the ground, not that he remains heavy and still levitates. The phenomenon of levitation does not appear to violate the basic laws of physics.

13.3 The Practice

Patanjali suggests that the issues related to physical health, stresses and strains are also obstacles to progress. To address these issues, Asanas (yoga postures) and Pranayam (breathing exercises) are suggested. Each sutra is studied on a regular basis until its meaning and significance are internalized. An operative word or a small group of words called *Beej Mantra* (Root word(s)) reflective of the meaning of the sutra are selected for meditation. Then, whenever the selected word(s) are chanted, the meaning of the entire sutra will fill our consciousness. This type of meditation is based on mantras and therefore, sound assumes importance. There are said to be four types of sound depicted in Figure 13.2 (Chitre, 2014). At the minimum, mantras should be chanted in *Madyama*, preferably near the upper boundary of *Pashyanti*. With practice, this should be possible. For ready reference, the program may be summarized is as follows:

1. Select the outcomes desirous of materialization.
2. Study the Patanjali's yoga sutras, Tirumular's Tirumantiram, or Durga Saptashati and identify a reasonable number of sutras/mantras to include in the meditation program.
3. Internalize the meaning of these sutras/mantras so when a specific sutra/mantra is chanted, the consciousness knows its meaning.
4. Select one or two operative words from each sutra/mantra which when chanted will cause the associated meaning to reach the deepest recesses of our consciousness.

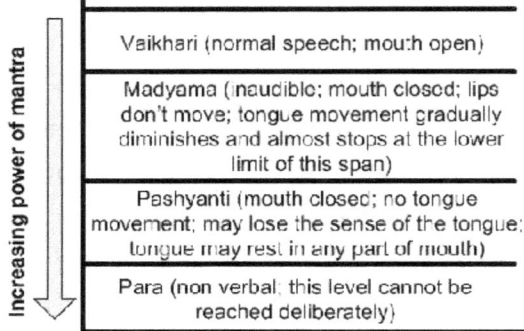

Figure 13. 2 Mantra and Sound

5. Select the chronology, power (Figure 13.2), and duration of each sutra/mantra, and duration of the program.
6. Select the physical exercises and breathing exercises to include for removing stresses and strains to ready the body for meditation.
7. Practice the meditation program for the duration of the program.
8. Evaluate the program efficacy; remember it may take an unspecified amount of time before the intended outcomes materialize. Six sigma principles need to be adhered to in all aspects of the program except during the meditative practice when total surrender is the key to success. Rational thinking is definitely an obstacle to success during the actual practice of meditation.
9. Be sure to secure the approval of your healthcare professional and physician. Soft seating such as mattresses needs to be in place; landing on hard surfaces could cause serious injury. Remember, you are undertaking the investigation entirely at Your Own Risk!

13. 4 Results

Sanjeev Aroskar gathered a group of seven participants in Pune, India for this investigation. They practiced their meditation program for nearly four months culminating in the final set of sessions on January 25 – 26, 2014. The first author had arrived in Pune in November 2013 for interactions with the participants. The first author shot a video of the session and the screenshots of five participants lifting off the ground to a varying degree are shown in Figure 13.3. Of the seven participants, six lifted off the ground on 25-26 January 2014 to varying levels ranging from a couple of inches to several feet. This is simply not possible unless the intention of lifting off the ground had materialized. None of the participants remained still in the air unlike the first author's mother who was seen in a stationary state some six to nine inches from the ground by the first author's older sister Vijaya 'Taii' Bhalerao in Pune when she was a teenager. Taii holds a BA from the University of Poona. Her daughter, Poornima Talwalker of Mumbai who has a Master's degree in psychology and Taii's son Sanjeev Bhalerao, an advertising executive in New Delhi with an MBA and a degree in Law told the first author that they too had witnessed their grandmother in a levitated state as young children. None of them knew what mantras the first author's mother was silently chanting but the family believes she had a pretty high S component. She died in 1997 at the age of 95 and for over seven prior decades must have completed hundreds of thousands of rounds of Japamala (rosary) daily.

166 | *Chapter 13. Meditation for Materialization of Intentions*

The first author interviewed of the participants on January 25th at the concluding session to learn of their experiences.

Figure 13.3. Five of the Participants Lifting from the Ground while in Meditation

Interview with Participants. The response of Dr. Rajiv Shelar MD (Orthopedics) in his own words:

I have experienced total happiness in my entire self. Usually, we experience happiness at the level of the mind but the body doesn't feel it or we have a bodily happy experience but the mind doesn't feel it. Now, the experience is in unison and I notice that my entire being is like a child bubbling with joy. After completion of the program I felt that I am dancing like I used to in my childhood.

One participant said, *My confidence level and positivity have improved. I felt like crying but not out of sorrow and then I felt peace afterwards.* Another commented, *I realize improvement in myself, there is peace in my family. My friends ask, what are you doing different*? A third comment was *My creativity has increased.* Additionally, everyone reported feeling better.

Finally, Maharishi's group had conducted multitude of investigations successfully delivering the intermediate results of levitation they call yogic flying based on their own method involving hundreds of thousands of participants (see for example the YouTube video at http://www.youtube.com/watch?v=jlw8CxTkyxA). Among the followers of Maharishi are numerous scientists such as renowned quantum physicist, John Hagelin, PhD, neurophysiologist Dr. R. Keith Wallace, PhD, and neuroscientist, Tony Nader, MD, PhD, and many celebrities such as the Beatles, film maker David Lynch, comedian Jerry Seinfeld, and scores of others.

Further Reading

[1] Belak, Tony and Curtin, J-R, Planned New U of L-Spalding Institute will Examine How Compassion Can Boost Business Performance, The Lane Report, August 5, 2013.

[2] Boyers, J., Why Empathy is the Force that Moves a Business Forward, Forbes, May 30, 2013.

[3] Chitre, Nitin, Private Communication, Pune, 10 January 2014.

[4] Deshpande, P. B. and Kulkarni, B. D., The Brahma Uncertainty Principle, Journal of Consciousness Exploration and Research, 3, 2, February 2012.

[5] Deshpande, P. B., and Kulkarni, B. D., and Aroskar S. S., and Bhavsar S. N., Levitation during Meditation: A Scientific Investigation, Journal of Consciousness Exploration and Research, 2, 4, June 2011.

[6] Deshpande, P. B., Six Sigma for Karma Capitalism, Six Sigma and Advanced Controls, Inc., 2011.

[7] Deshpande, P. B. and Christopher, P. M., On The Cyclical Nature of Excellence, Reflections, Vol. 1, No. 1, 1993.

[8] DeSteno, David, The Morality of Meditation, Op Ed Column, NY Times, July 5, 2013 (Condon, Paul, et al., J Psychological Science, 21 August 2013). This paper shows how meditation directly leads to more compassion

[9] Fryer, B., The Rise of Compassionate Management (Finally), Harvard Business School Blog Network, September 18, 2013.

[10] George Bill, Compassion Makes You a Better Leader, Harvard Professor George's Blog, 2013.

[11] Govindan, Marshall, Kriya Yoga Sutras of Patanjali and the Siddhas, Babaji's Kriya Yoga Order of Acharyas Trust, Bangalore, India (2003).
[12] Korotkov K.G., Energy Fields Eletrophotonic Analysis in Humans and Nature, 2012. 240 p. e-book: Amazon.com.
[13] Mannikar, T. G., Samkhyakarika of Isvarakrsna, Oriental Book Agency, Poona, 2nd Printing 1972.
[14] Thakur, Nanda and Thakur Jitendranath, Sarth Shridurgasaptashati 5th Ed., Dharmic Publication House, Mumbai 2013.
[15] Tiller, W. A., Psychoenergetic Science: Second Copernican Revolution, www.amazon.com, 2007.
[16] Tiller, W. A. and Dibble, W. E., White Paper II: Steps for Moving Psychoenergetic Science into the Hands of General Public Researchers, 2009 (www.tiller.org).
[17] Wallace, R. K., Physiological Effects of Transcendental Meditation, Science, Vol. 167, No. 3926, 1970.

CHAPTER 14
Why Six Sigma

This chapter provides a more detailed explanation for the need for six sigma scrutiny in the quest for internal excellence. Six sigma was created at Motorola by Bill Smith and Mikel Harry in the late seventies at a time when the company revenues had plummeted to $2 billion raising serious concern among the top management. A decade after six sigma implementation, the company revenues jumped to $8 billion earning Motorola the inaugural Malcolm Baldrige National Quality Award from president Regan in 1988. By now, over 40% of US corporations and organizations and multitude of companies overseas have embraced six sigma. However, what is not appreciated in some quarters is that six sigma is not just another quality initiative but a fundamental approach to problem solving that is founded on sound natural laws.

Six sigma is a fundamental approach to problem solving that is based solely on input-output data. In sciences and engineering disciplines such approaches are called systemic approaches. Fundamental, mechanistic approaches should always be preferred to systemic approaches but in the vast majority of processes of importance, such detailed fundamental knowledge of the system under scrutiny is unavailable.

Six sigma can deliver the best possible performance in all activities from wake up time to bed time. It is appropriate for simple or highly complex manufacturing or service processes, linear or nonlinear, static or dynamic. By best possible performance we mean the outcome exhibiting a minimum amount of variation statisticians refer to as common cause variability. Such variation arises due to unknown and uncontrollable causes, or so we thought until just a few years ago. The next chapter, Criticality of Internal Excellence in Six Sigma Programs, presents strong evidence that internal excellence can boost performance in all aspects of life beyond the common cause variability limit taking us to a new state where the defects are even lower. Still, zero defects ad infinitum is not in the plan of nature

The discovery of the link of internal excellence to six sigma has been a Eureka moment and is being reported in book form for the first time. It has profound implications for organizations and nations. The general conclusion is that internal excellence delivers great performance and when six sigma is introduced, exemplary performance results. It follows therefore, the absence of internal excellence *and* six sigma are an invitation to disaster.

Yoga is the science of internal excellence. The pursuit of internal excellence is itself a comprehensive six sigma problem provided we remember that during the practice of meditation, all rational thinking must come to an end. We humans are multivariable, nonlinear, self-regulating, and evolving with each having a unique common cause variability that we inherit from our ancestors and by own actions in this life.

There are many books on six sigma in the market by now. Two are cited in the References. Here we simply provide the rules of working smarter for they are important in the pursuit of internal excellence.

Do's and don'ts of Working Smarter. In the pursuit of internal excellence, an aspirant needs to adhere to a number of do's and don'ts of working smarter:

1. **Never skip any step.** Always follow the eleven-step six sigma methodology regardless of the problem you are working on in a disciplined manner relying on data (evidence) alone for decision-making and let the methodology suggest the path to improvement. Far too often, problems are articulated and solutions proposed more or less in the same breath, skipping the nine steps in between.
2. **Six sigma can handle every process or transaction**. Six sigma being a fundamental methodology for improving the performance of every process and transaction, highly complex work processes can be tackled. However, it is advisable to break up the processes into tractable pieces so the project can be completed in a reasonable amount of time.
3. **Correlation does not necessarily imply causality.** If there is a causality, there will always be a correlation but if there is correlation, there may or may not be causality. This happens because of the presence of 'lurking variables' (unknown causes). It is only with the six sigma methodology that you will determine whether there is a causal link between a perceived cause and an effect.

4. **Always validate measurement systems.** We cannot emphasize this enough. Errors due to measurement systems must be a small fraction of the variation (defects) in the outcome due to discoverable causes. Failure to do so can lead to catastrophic results. A Russian scientist reported some years back that in the cold war when he was the operational in-charge, the software detected an incoming nuclear missile. Had he followed the normal protocol, he would have initiated a nuclear response. Fortunately for us, he decided to ignore the protocol or lese we wouldn't be here to write this book. The ballot paper and machine problems in Dade County, Florida in the 2000 Presidential elections eventually led to the US Supreme Court deciding the results of the presidential election is another example. There are thousands of examples like this but do remember, never engage in finger-pointing; always aim at system improvements!

5. **Never rely on a single measurement for decision making.** Relying on a single measurement of the outcome before and after to assess improvement is problematic because the outcome has variation due to uncontrollable and unknown causes (common cause variability). It is best to work with averages, which have the effect of nullifying these variations to assess whether in fact there is an improvement.

6. **Homogeneous and Heterogeneous Populations.** Simple random sampling suffices for homogeneous populations but sometimes populations are heterogeneous populations in which case, stratified sampling must be used to determine the defect levels.

7. **Design of Experiments (DOE).** In DOE, all inputs are varied simultaneously and the data on the outcomes recorded for analysis. That said, let us remember, if you wish to assess the influence of a single input (cause) upon an outcome (effect), the other inputs must be held constant.
8. **When six sigma will not improve performance?** If someone asserts that their process cannot be improved, they are implicitly telling you that the entire variation in the outcome of their work process is due to uncontrollable causes. That reasoning is flawed because we only come to know how many of the defects are due to uncontrollable causes in hindsight, only after the six sigma project has been completed, not at the start.
9. This book being about internal excellence, there are a few more concepts to bear in mind. We humans are all nonlinear, self-regulating, multivariable, and evolving with a unique common cause variability that in six sigma terms due to our ancestry or in yogic terms due to our past karmas. Thus, six sigma projects involving internal excellence need to be handled with TLC. Refrain from extending the findings of a project to the wider population.

The wherewithal in this book will take an aspirant to a higher level of internal excellence. It is essential to adhere to six sigma principles in this pursuit but when we sit for meditation, the rational mind must be sent on a vacation. We have been warned by self- realized yogis that such separation is difficult but that is the nature of our training. If sufficient number from the 6 ½ billion were to embrace the science and practices of internal and external excellence, the world will be a far better place. Those few among us who wish to traverse the entire scale of the S, R, T level of consciousness towards enlightenment, self-realized yogis are your best bet but then be prepared to completely surrender.

References

[1] Deshpande, P. B., *Six Sigma for Karma Capitalism*, Six Sigma and Advanced Controls, Inc., 2011.

[2] Harry, J. Mikel and Lawson, J. R., *Six Sigma Productivity Analysis and Process Characterization*, Motorola Press, 1992.

CHAPTER 15
Criticality of Internal Excellence in Six Sigma Programs

Six sigma and its cousin Lean Six Sigma by now are mature frameworks having been embraced by over 40% of US domestic and multinational organizations including many US federal agencies. If embraced and diligently pursued, six sigma is quite capable of transforming entire nations, not just corporations. This assertion is based on the capacity of six sigma to operate all human activities, manufacturing or transactional (service), linear or nonlinear, static or dynamic, in the best possible manner, maximizing quality and customer satisfaction, and minimizing cycle times, minimizing energy consumption, and defects. It is unwise to think of six sigma as yet another quality initiative. It is also a way of thinking, a way of problem-solving, using data and strict discipline. All that remains true today. So if someone had asked us a few years ago, *Is six sigma the ultimate in excellence*? Or put it another way, *Beyond six sigma what*? we really did not have a good answer but now we do! What has changed is that a considerable body of evidence has come to light leading us to assert that while six sigma is necessary for excellence, it is not sufficient for breakthrough performance. The elephant in the room is the level of internal excellence. In the absence of internal excellence, six sigma performs (for that matter, any other quality initiative be it TQM, Kaizen, Lean, CMM Level 5, Balanced Score Card, etc.) will fall far short of expectations. Put it another way, in the presence of internal excellence, six sigma programs will lead to exemplary performance. By extension, the absence of both components of excellence is an invitation to disaster.

15.1 Internal Excellence Boosts Business Performance

At the conclusion of his first interview with the New York Times (21 February 2014), Satya Nadella, the then newly appointed CEO of Microsoft remarked, *One of the things I am fascinated about generally is the rise and fall of everything, from civilizations, to families, to companies. We all know the mortality of companies is less than human beings. There are few examples of even 100-year old companies. For us to be a 100-year-old company where people find meaning at work, that is the quest.*

The scientific framework for individual, organizational, national, and world transformation is the path forward to realize Mr. Nadella's vision. Rise and fall of civilizations follow certain natural laws, however, as we have pointed out there is nothing in these laws to suggest that with deliberate intent, emerging nations such as India cannot rise faster, or nations currently in decline such as Greece cannot change direction, or for that matter, developed nations such as the United States cannot keep decline at bay longer. Furthermore, these laws apply to populations at large placing no limit whatsoever on individuals aspiring to rise to the highest level possible for a human being regardless of where on the rise and decline curve their civilization happens to be. These ideas extend to companies as well.

In the following paragraphs three examples are presented to substantiate the claim of a strong link of internal excellence to exemplary performance: (1) Mumbai's Dabbawallas, (2) The 2013 Kumbh Mela, and (3) Gamarra Businesses of Lima, Peru.

15.2. Mumbai's Dabbawallas (Lunchbox delivery boys)

Mumbai's Dabbawallas are 5,000-strong internationally-renowned lunchbox delivery boys reportedly with an average eighth grade education who deliver some 150,000 lunch boxes a day in Mumbai, India. Figure 15.1 shows a couple of Dabbawallas at work. Each day, the lunch boxes containing home-cooked meals are picked up from the residences of customers who commute to the city-center and delivered to their offices. The lunch boxes are picked up from customers' homes long after they have left for work. After lunch, the process is reversed. Let us say the lunch box delivery time is 12:30 PM and the empty boxes are picked up at 1:30 PM for the return journey and delivered before the customers return. The Dabbawallas know that customer satisfaction issues arise if a customer receives someone else's lunch box or if it does not arrive on time. These Dabbawallas reportedly make one mistake every two months or so. That's an error rate of one in 8 million deliveries. So impressed was Britain's Prince Charles that he paid them a personal visit to witness their operations. The price for this exemplary service is about $3 per month. In a 1998 article, Forbes expressed their feelings this way: *Superb service and*

180 | *Chapter 15. Criticality of Internal Excellence in Six Sigma*

Figure 15.1. Dabbawallas at Work

charity too. Can anyone ask for more? The Dabbawallas themselves believe, *Work is worship*. The author has been talking up this example in his six sigma training programs for over a decade challenging students that such a great performance is possible when six sigma practices are followed. There is no doubt the performance is outstanding and that the process is six sigma compliant but the claim now is that such performance is impossible without a sufficiently high S component. In late June 2014 the first author and his wife went to see the Bollywood film Lunch Box not knowing what to expect other than the knowledge it had been screened at the 2013 Cannes Film Festival and later had won the Critics Week Viewers' Choice Award also known as Grand Rail d'Or. A few scenes into the film, it became clear that the movie was inspired by Mumbai's Dabbawallas. The plot is about how wrongful delivery of two lunch boxes turns into an interesting storyline. I was thrilled to see the evidence of internal excellence play out on the big screen.

15.2. The 2013 Kumbh Mela

Kumbh Mela, believed to be the largest religious gathering of humans on earth is held at in the city of Allahabad in the state of Uttar Pradesh in India every twelve years on the banks of the confluence of the holy rivers Ganga, Yamuna, and the mythical Saraswati. Most recently the Mela was celebrated during the first quarter of 2013. The Financial Times carried an interesting article on March 1, 2013 written by Victor Mallet titled, *Pop-up Mega City is a Lesson in Logistics for India* along with a photograph of the tent city in Figure 15. 2.

Figure 15.2. Tent Mega City at the Kumbh (Source: Financial Times)

Said the Financial Times article, to somebody who does projects, the tent city is like a mega-refugee camp that comes up overnight and gets sustained and managed for two months with people filtering in and out at a rate of millions a day.

It's managed by the Uttar Pradesh State government. If somehow we could translate that capacity to day-to-day business, you could transform UP. It's really a powerful thought. Uttar Pradesh is often seen as the epitome of all that is wrong with India. With a population of over 200 million – larger than Brazil's – the state is notoriously corrupt and inefficient. Take sanitation. In the decade to 2011, the UP government reported steadily rising construction of latrines in rural areas with the help of $600 million in public funds. But the 2011 census showed that almost no toilets had actually been built. Most of the money was stolen, leaving tens of thousands of children to die each year as a result of diarrhea spread by what one aid worker called appalling sanitation. There are few such problems at the Kumbh Mela, however.

Mr. Onno Ruhl, Head of the World Bank in India, who visited the Kumbh Mela was so moved by the operations that he decided to bathe in the Ganges himself. He called it an incredible logistical operation. Said Mr. Ruhl in the Financial Times article, The city on the sandbanks, soon to be dismantled before the river floods, "has water, sanitation, power, and solid-waste management, everything, actually, that many Indian cities lack.

Harvard researchers described it as a *pop-up mega city*. The bureaucrats and workers from Uttar Pradesh, India's most populous and one of the poorest states took less than three months to build a tent city for 2 million residents complete with hard roads, toilets, running water, electricity, food shops, garbage collection, and well-manned police stations. This year's event attracted millions of pilgrims from across

India who came to wash away their sins in the Ganges at its confluence with the Yamuna. Over its two months to mid-March, the Mela attracted 80 -100 million visitors, with up to 30 million attempting to bathe in the river on February 10 alone, officials say. Precise numbers are hard to come by but the devotees and foreign visitors are generally full of praise for the organizers of what is arguably the largest gathering of humans on earth. Apart from a February 10 stampede at the nearby Allahabad railway station in which 36 were killed, the Kumbh Mela itself has so far gone off smoothly. Fresh water comes out of the taps, toilets are disinfected, trained police carefully shepherd the crowds to the bathing areas, and the lights come on at night.

Devesh Chaturvedi, Divisional commissioner of Allahabad is proud of the huge task that he and perhaps 100,000 workers completed in organizing the festival. He mentions 165 km of roads on the sand made of steel plates, 18 pontoon bridges, 560 km of water supply lines, 670 km of electricity lines, 22,500 street lights and 200,000 electricity connections, as well as 275 food shops for essential supplies such as flour, rice, milk and cooking gas. Mr. Chaturvedi agrees there is a contrast between the successful provision of these services and the way life continues in the rest of the state, and has two explanations. First, the authorities ensure that all those working on the project are accountable for their actions and the money they spend. Second, those involved are highly motivated. They feel it's a real service to all these pilgrims who have come here, the sadhus [holy men] and the seers, so it's a sort of mission which motivates them to work extra, despite difficult working conditions.

In the concluding thoughts on the article, Victor writes, a question on the minds of both Indians and foreigners: How? Why? Or rather: if the authorities can build infrastructure so efficiently for this short but very large festival and its instant city, why can't they do the same for permanent villages and towns? We trust the answer is clear to the readers of this article. This level of performance would have been impossible in the absence of a high level of consciousness on the part of both the workers and devotees.

15.3. Gamarra Businesses of Peru

Gamarra businesses span 34 blocks around Hipólito Unanue and Agustín Gamarra streets in La Victoria region of Lima, Peru. Gamarra has 25,000 businesses that employ 100,000 workers, generating $1.2 billion in revenue annually. These businesses import textiles from several countries at competitive prices. Depending on the size, individual entrepreneurs are set up to handle a certain volume of business. However, by agreements with other entrepreneurs they can handle orders of any size up to the total capacity of all entrepreneurs in Gamarra. This arrangement assures B-to-B customers of not only high quality and low cost but also a quick turnaround.

Depending on the season, anywhere between 150,000 and 600,000 people visit Gamarra every day. Seventy percent of visitors reportedly purchase something or the other. Gamarra entrepreneurs are renowned and widely respected among both business customers and end-use consumers. Their textile products are known for high quality and low cost.

Chapter 15. Criticality of Internal Excellence in Six Sigma

The author visited Gamarra in 2008 with his former doctoral scholar, Dr. Roberto Z. Tantalean to study their operations from a lean six sigma perspective (see Figure 15.3). Like their counterparts in Mumbai, they are not a highly educated workforce. That theirs is a lean six sigma operation is absolutely clear; nothing goes to waste and there is a very high level of customer satisfaction. A clue to their higher S component is their motto, *Compete but cooperate*!

Figure 15.3. The First Author and his Peruvian associate, Dr. Roberto Z. Tantalean at Gamarra

Acknowledgments

This chapter is an extended adaptation of a column the first author wrote with Dr. Mikel Harry, co-creator of six sigma.

References

[1] Deshpande, P. B. and Harry, M., Criticality of Internal Excellence in Six Sigma for National Transformation, Unpublished 2014.
[2] Deshpande, P. B., *Six Sigma for Karma Capitalism*, Six Sigma and Advanced Controls, Inc., 2011.
[3] Harry, J. Mikel and Lawson, J. R., *Six Sigma Productivity Analysis and Process Characterization*, Motorola Press, 1992.

CHAPTER 16

Collective Consciousness for World Peace

At first glance this may appear to be a nearly impossible task given that the world population is 6 ½ billion and rising. The theory of rise and decline precludes global peace on a permanent basis since different societies are always in the depth of decline while the rest are in the various stages of rise and decline. However, with the present framework it should be possible to make the world more peaceful. For example, consider the current state of three nations, namely Greece, India, and the US depicted in Figure 16.1. The figure shows all three types of societies that will be found at any given time: risen, rising, and in decline.

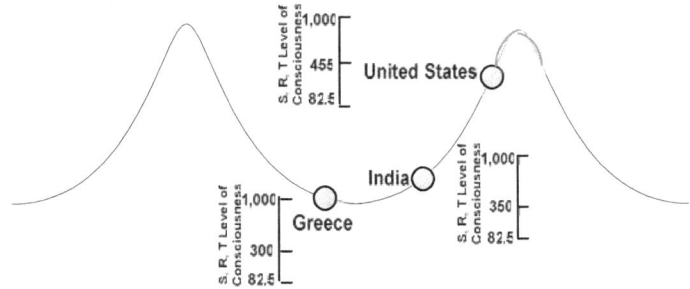

Figure 16.1 Rise and Decline of Greece, India and the United States

After making phenomenal contributions to human civilization, India declined in its last cycle over two thousand years ago and is now rising again. The United States is thought to be somewhere in the region marked in heavy font in Figure 16.1. Only in hindsight would we know for sure where the US was at this point in time. The calibrations for the US and India in Figure 16.1 are due to the late Dr. David R. Hawkins, MD reported in his book Power vs. Force. So powerful is the theory of rise and decline that the very culture whose wisdom led the theory itself finds calibrated considerably lower than the United States. The first author has been going to Greece for nine years to teach a two-week six sigma program for the MBA students of the University of Kentucky at TEI/Piraeus in Athens Greece. The average level of consciousness of Greece is his estimate. The challenge for Greece is to change direction, for India to accelerate its rise, and for the US to sustain rise, keep decline at bay longer.

To understand how the present framework may contribute to a more just and peaceful world, we must first understand the notion of collective human consciousness and as a subset, certain attributes of non-human living systems and inanimate systems that are physically linked. Consider a set of metronomes placed on a wooden plank atop two empty soda cans. Now, select a certain frequency of oscillation for the metronomes, wind them up, hold the arm of each at a different starting position, and let them oscillate. You will see that the metronomes synchronize quickly. For a You Tube demonstration of this experiment, visit

http://www.youtube.com/watch?v=01_Lii68ZzI.

Chapter 16. Collective Consciousness for World Peace

Of course, in this instance the metronomes are physically linked via the freely moving base in a way that facilitates energy transfer among them. But such a phenomena can occur among living systems, including humans.

Take the example of a non-human living system first. The Late Dr. Lewis Thomas, MD Harvard University who was President of Memorial Sloan-Kettering Cancer Center in New York wrote in his book, The Lives of a Cell that termites with some 50,000 neurons in their heads are hardly able to do anything individually much less think. However, in a colony of tens of thousands of termites, *thinking begins and they wind up building colonies containing symmetrical columns and beautiful arches.* This example is indicative of the enormous intelligence of collective consciousness.

Now, let us take two examples of collective human consciousness. The first involves an experiment called Global Consciousness Project that Professor Roger Nelson and his team of Princeton University researchers direct. Under the auspices of this project, over one hundred electronic random number generators (RNGs) have been installed in different parts of the world of which fifty to sixty are operational at any given time. Under normal circumstances the RNG network produces a completely unpredictable sequences of zeros and ones but when the collective human consciousness becomes coherent/synchronizes because of a great event, good or bad, natural or man-made, the network of RNGs outputs becomes structured, i. e., it quits producing random numbers. The researchers peg the probability that the observed effect being due to chance at one in a billion. Figure 16.2(a) depicts the

RNG output at the time of the September 11, 2001 terrorist attacks on the World Trade Center in New York. Notice that the changes in the RNG outputs at the time of the attacks are rather large. Even more intriguing is the observation that the changes in RNG Output occurred several hours before the attacks as though human consciousness knows things that it is not aware of.

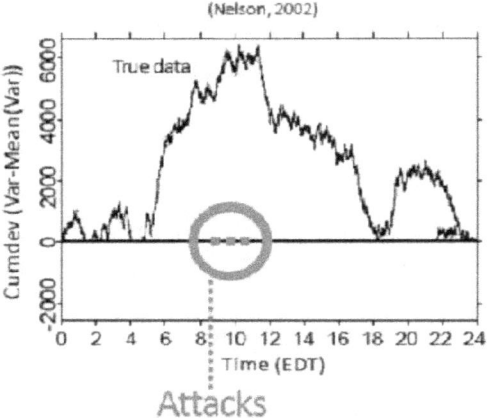

Figure 16.2(a). RNG Output at the time of 9/11 (Source noosphere.princeton.edu)

Increasing global consciousness translates into increasing randomness of the RNG outputs and promote peaceful conditions while the opposite is the case when the randomness decreases. Global unrest is linked with reducing randomness of the network output.

Collective consciousness and collective coherence are synonymous. The second example involves a project called Global Coherence Monitoring System (GCMS) based on a network of magnetometers. The non-profit Institute for HeartMath in California runs this project in cooperation with renowned astrophysicist and nuclear scientist Elizabeth

Rauscher, PhD. The GCMS measures fluctuations in the magnetic fields generated by the earth and in the ionosphere. The central idea is that the earth's magnetic field changes in response to significant global events. As one example of the efficacy of GCMS, Drs. Rauscher and her late husband Dr. Van Bise predicted the cataclysmic eruption of Mount St. Helens in the state of Washington on May 18, 1980. These researchers postulate that GCMS is sensitive to the effects of emotion-based human interactions. For example, two National Oceanic and Atmospheric space weather satellites monitoring the Earth's magnetic field also displayed a significant spike at the time of the 9/11 attacks and for several days thereafter. These data are depicted in Figure 16.2(b).

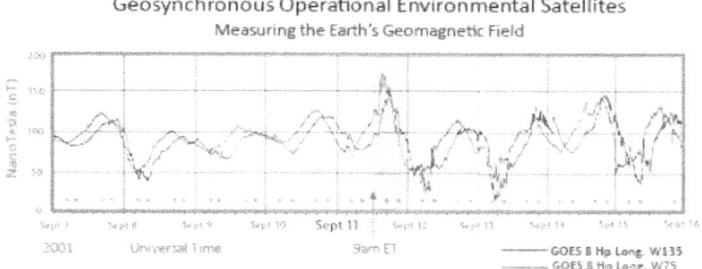

Figure 16.2(b). Geosynchronous Operational Environmental Satellites Measuring the Earth's Magnetic Field at the Time of 9/11 Attacks (Source Courtesy, IHM)

These two projects merely record the correlates of global consciousness/coherence and significant global events but the obvious extension is to direct global consciousness/coherence to improve humanity and that is a feedback control problem. How to convince national Governments and International bodies such as the United

Nations to embark on a global meditation initiative would have been a formidable task just a couple of decades ago but may be not beyond reach now. Even when we succeed in doing so, it is not clear how many of the 6 ½ billion inhabitants of Earth would voluntarily undertake to meditate twice daily not only for themselves but also for humanity at large. Fortunately, there is a way out and this is where the phenomenal work of the late Maharishi Mahesh Yogi and his associates assumes significance. The Late Maharishi Mahesh Yogi put forward an idea several decades ago which has come to be known as the Maharishi effect. The Maharishi effect states that global peace requires a mere $\sqrt{1\%}$ of the people meditating on a regular basis. For a world population of 6.5 billion this number works out to be roughly 8,000. Many outstanding scientists were subscribers to his transcendental meditation program and there is a university in Fairfield, Iowa named in his name. His associates have carried out many experiments to demonstrate the Maharishi effect.

A team of scientists affiliated with the Maharishi organization carried out an experiment in the Middle East in the eighties to assess the efficacy of the Maharishi effect in Lebanon and Israel. Orme-Johnson and David Leffler conducted an experiment during the peak of the Israel-Lebanon war in the 1980s and found that the larger the number of meditators, the more marked was the reduced level of conflict. They also found improvement in crime, auto accidents, fires, national mood, etc. (Orme-Johnson, et al., 1988).

Maharishi follower and renowned quantum physicist John Hagelin, PhD and his associates conducted another experiment to demonstrate the benefit of group meditation. In this experiment 4,000 meditators meditated daily for a period of eight weeks during June 7 - July 30, 1993 to increase coherence and reduce stress in Washington DC with the intention to bring down the crime rate in the District of Columbia (Hagelin, et al., 1999). The authors reported that a twenty-seven-member Review Board consisting of sociologists and criminologists from leading universities, representatives from the police department and the Government of the District of Columbia, together with civic leaders approved the research protocol for the project in advance and monitored progress. The outcome selected for assessment was the Weekly Crime Rate as measured by the Uniform Crime Report program of the Federal Bureau of Investigation. The results of this experiment are shown in Figure 16.3.

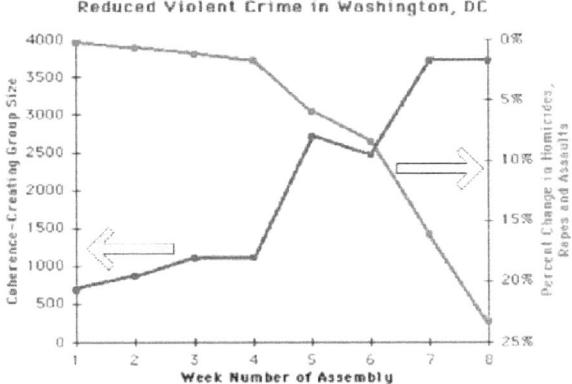

Figure 16.3. Efficacy of TM Siddhi™ Program in DC (With Permission of Dr. John Hagelin)

These results suggest a causal link between societal stress, lack of collective coherence, and unrest. Reduce stress and the world will become more peaceful. The telomere investigations of Nobel-Prize winning scientist Elizabeth Blackburn, PhD and the bioenergy investigations of Konstantin Korotkov, PhD, cited in earlier chapters are consistent with the findings in this chapter. Furthermore, Vedic/yogic wisdom is supportive of the work.

The first author is a chemical engineer specializing in advanced control and optimization and six sigma. In industrial practice, constrained model predictive control remains the state of the art. We could think of the problem of promoting global peace as a feedback control problem. Here, the controlled variable is the randomness of two outputs: RNGs and Magnetometer network outputs. The target is "Increasing randomness of the outputs". The unmeasured disturbances are *Significant global events*. The control algorithm is *Group meditation*. The manipulated variables are (1) Number of meditators, and (2) Duration of meditation. Thus, with a sufficiently large number of people meditating for global peace, decreasing randomness of the signal is indicative of impending disaster and would prompt a control action consisting of enlisting a larger number of people to sit for meditation and/or increasing the duration of meditation. Rising randomness of the outputs is the desired direction.

To summarize

This chapter has presented strong rationale for the power of collective human consciousness to bring about changes to make this a more peaceful world. Scientific evidence and ancient wisdom are both supportive of the assertion.

Further Reading

[1] Global Consciousness Project, http://noosphere.princeton.edu
[2] Global Coherence Initiative, www.glcoherence.org.
[3] Hagelin, John, The Power of the Collective, The Mystique of Intention – Shift! At the Frontiers of Consciousness, No. 15, June – August 2007.
[4] Hagelin, John S., et al., Effects of Group Practice of the Transcendental Meditation Program on Preventing Violent Crime in Washington, DC: Results of the National Demonstration Project, June-July 1993, Social Indicators Research, 47, 2, 153-201, 1999.
[5] Orme-Johnson, David W., International Peace Project in the Middle East – The Effects of Maharishi Technology of the United Field, Journal of Conflict Resolution, 32, 1988 pp 776-812.

CHAPTER 17
Interfaith Understanding and Racial Harmony

In this chapter we consider several more important topics: Interfaith Understanding, racial harmony, nuclear weapons, and when democracy is apt to deliver the desired results. The theory of rise and decline provides the answer to all three queries.

17.1 Interfaith Understanding

Out of vibrations is born energy, out of energy the ultimate reality, cosmic consciousness, and out of cosmic consciousness the physical reality, this universe. This book has been all about connecting to this consciousness, identifying the obstacles to progress, and outlining the processes with which to reach the goal. When we succeed, we emerge as an individual of higher consciousness, internal excellence. And along the way, we would derive myriad of other benefits.

We have presented two pathways for progress: The first is a conscious approach in which we watch over our S, R, T components to ensure that S remains high or nudges higher and R and T stay at reasonable levels and perhaps nudge lower. The second pathway involves a process whose side effect is a rise in the level of consciousness, level of internal excellence. Meditation is suggested as the wherewithal for achieving this goal. However, this is not a religious pursuit. Individuals of four different faiths have made this scientific framework possible. Separation of church and state is a precious concept worth nurturing.

So why do so many problems arise on account of religion? Religious intolerance is ostensibly the most serious threat to global peace. By now you are intimately familiar with the link of S, R, T Level of consciousness and emotions. Positive emotions strongly correlate with the S component and negative emotions with excessive R and T components. In his talks on Internal Excellence in several countries the first author asks the audiences to opine on who might be towards the top of the scale, invariably they take such names as Mother Theresa, Mahatma Gandhi, Martin Luther King, etc. When asked to ponder who might be even higher, the answer comes back, Jesus, Buddha, Krishna, Prophet Mohammed, etc. And, who might be at the bottom, the names of Hitler, bin Laden, Stalin, etc., come up. When asked where they might be on this scale, they uniformly agree, somewhere in between the two extremes. And finally when asked which direction they ought to try to go in their lifetime, they all respond, up!

So, why has there been so much violence in the name of religion? Because, some human beings take their view of God as the only true interpretation and their incarnation or Prophet as the only one at the top of the scale and that the only way for everyone else to progress is through their messenger. When such individuals are endowed with excessive R and T components it spells trouble for humanity. This is true today as it has been in the past. It is neither wise nor possible to rank-order the messengers for three reasons: (1) it implies the ability to discern truth from falsehood. Our study indicates that only individuals at a very high level of consciousness possess such an ability and they would never use it to harm anyone. (2) As the Late Dr. David R. Hawkins would put it, *"Every level of consciousness has an understanding of reality that is valid only at that level of perception"*. Given that there is widespread agreement we are way down from the top end of the scale of consciousness, most of us simply do not have the capacity to grasp what the reality is. (3) Let us not forget, the messages of incarnations, Prophet, son of God, etc., are nearly identical! The authors of this book were born in two different faiths.

A sage once observed, *"Whenever there is a decline of righteousness and the rise of wickedness, a messenger is born to put humanity back on the path of righteousness"*. You can easily translate the counsel of the sage to mean when the T component of a society gains dominance it eventually gives way to the rise of the S component. This is a universal concept. A study of the scriptures of various faiths reveals striking similarities between the teachings of the respective masters. For example, author and biblical scholar Marcus Borg found the striking similarities between the sayings of Buddha and Jesus to be eerie. These ideas tell us that every one of the masters was trying to raise the S component of the societies in which they were born.

17.2 Racial Harmony

The theory of rise and decline posits that the rise and decline are natural processes and although they are slow processes, no society is immune to them. To harbor a sense of racial superiority because their society is in the risen state at the present time is problematic because decline is inevitable. This understanding should lead us to shun any sense of superiority on the basis of race.

The four-fold Varna system (Brahmin. Kshatriya, Vaishya, and Shudra) in the Indian context was born out of the three components called Gunas (S, R, T) thousands of years ago, there wasn't even a hint at the time that the Varnas could be inherited. But this is precisely how it has been practiced for two thousand years or more in spite of the clear evidence to the contrary. If you guessed the rising T components during the declining phase of India is the culprit you be absolutely right.

17.3 Nuclear Weapons

Nuclear weapons in the possession of a society in the depth of decline can be disastrous. So, the global efforts aimed at keeping certain societies from developing such weapons are understandable. But the question is about risen and rising societies which possess nuclear weapons now. What happens when these societies decline and remain in the possession of nuclear weapons?

17.4 Is Democracy Right for Everyone?

The concept of democracy is widely admired. Here, we wish to shed additional light on it. Democracy is so widely admired because we presume that democratic societies adhere to certain grounding principles leading to the outcomes identified in Figure 17.1. Now let us refresh our understanding of why societies rise and decline. Figure 17.2 is a reproduction of the diagram presented earlier in the chapter on theory of rise and decline. Here the average S, R, T level of consciousness of the society under scrutiny is depicted as the vertical line on the skewed Bell curve. So, when will democracy deliver the intended outcomes identified in Figure 17.1?

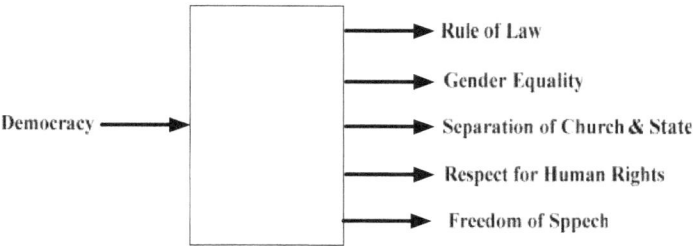

Figure 17.1 Democracy as an Input Output System

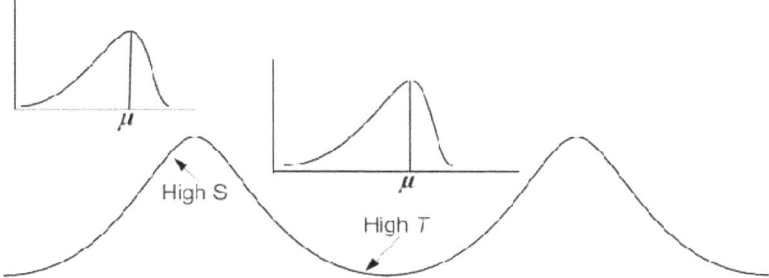

Figure 17.2 Rise and Decline of Societies

Let us revisit Figure 17.1 this time for a society in the depth of decline as shown in Figure 17.3. Clearly, in the society where the average T component is high, democracy cannot be expected to deliver the intended outcomes. The evidence

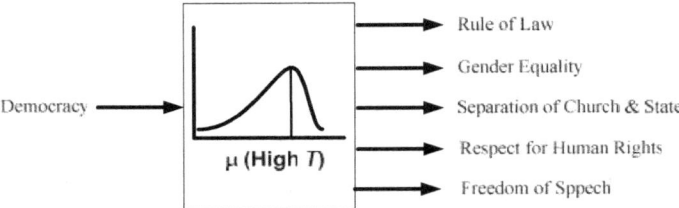

Figure 17.3 Democracy in a Society in Decline

of the correctness of the hypothesis is overwhelming. Take the United States for example and ask the question, how old the democracy is. Most will say over two hundred years old. In 1976 this country celebrated the bicentennial. But if you take democracy to also mean the majority of the population will determine how a nation is governed and the outcomes shown in Figure 17.1 are guaranteed to everyone, it will be quickly clear, US democracy is not that old. Women were granted the right to vote in 1920 and although African Americans were granted the right to vote in 1870, they were by and large kept out of the process until much later. While it is clear where democracy is apt to succeed, it is not clear what the alternative is for societies that are in the depth of decline.

Further Reading

1. **Borg, Marcus**, Ed., Jesus and Buddha: Parallel Sayings, Ulysses Press, Berkeley, CA 1997.
2. **Deshpande, P. B.**, Democracy, Religion, and Terrorism: A Perspective, Unpublished, 2006.

CHAPTER 18

Science and Spirituality: A Perfect Standoff

This the final chapter of the book discusses the scientific basis for spirituality in the context of a recent book by Amanda Gefter (2014). Her book demonstrates why there is an impasse in the reconciliation of science with spirituality. This impasse is about the nature of reality, specifically what we mean by *reality*, and about our basic assumptions about the nature of the world, the nature of consciousness, and the nature of the ultimate reality underlying both the world and consciousness, which is summed up with the slogan, *Nothing is ultimately real*.

In her paradigm-shattering recent book, as it surveys the landscape of modern physics, Amanda Gefter (2014) draws the astounding conclusion that *Nothing is ultimately real*. By *ultimate reality*, Gefter refers to what is invariant and the same for all observers. She relentlessly demonstrates that modern physics conclusively shows that everything in the world, including the world itself, is "radically observer-dependent", and therefore cannot ultimately be real.

Gefter demonstrates that the only "thing" that is ultimately real is the *primordial nothingness*, which is infinite, unbounded and undifferentiated. An observable world only appears within this primordial nothingness when a boundary arises within its midst and encodes information. She correctly identifies the observer of that world as a frame of reference, specifically the central point of view of that reference frame, but also shows that even this reference frame is not ultimately real, since the reference frame can only arise together with the observable world perceived in that frame of reference. That observable world is always defined in terms of the information encoded on a boundary that surrounds the observer at the central point of view of that reference frame.

Gefter describes the origin of the observer's world can only arise when a boundary arises that limits observations in the observer's frame of reference. She concludes that both the observable world, which arises in terms of the information encoded on a boundary arising in a reference frame, and the observer of that world, arising at the central point of view of that reference frame, are illusions. The only *thing* that is ultimately real and is not an illusion is the *primordial nothingness*, within which both the surrounding boundary and the central point of view arise.

If we call the observer at the central point of view a *focal point of consciousness*, we then conclude that both this differentiated focal point of consciousness and the observable world it perceives, as defined in terms of the information encoded on the boundary surrounding the focal point, are ultimately unreal. The only *thing* that is ultimately real is the *primordial nothingness*, which is infinite, unbounded and undifferentiated.

Chapter 18. Science and Spirituality: A Perfect Standoff

Is it possible that an observable world and the consciousness that observes that world are both illusions? It is common in neuroscience (Damasio, 1999) to assume that the world is real, while the consciousness that perceives that world is understood to be something of an illusion, but can both the perceivable world and the perceiving consciousness be illusions?

How can *nothing* be ultimately real? Doesn't the *primordial nothingness* have to have some inherent attributes of both a perceivable world, which arises within itself in terms of the information encoded on a boundary, and the focal point of perceiving consciousness, which arises at the central point of view of that boundary? How can we understand these attributes? Does it make any sense to understand this ultimate reality as pure *nothingness*?

This chapter, which is a summary of a much fuller article (Kowall and Deshpande, 2014) reviews the scientific evidence for the conclusions Gefter draws, but also argues for the inherent nature of the *primordial nothingness* beyond what Gefter describes as infinite, unbounded and undifferentiated. The bottom line of this investigation is that the *primordial nothingness* must have the nature of an *empty space of potentiality* that is the source of all physical energy and information characterizing any world, and is also a *void of undifferentiated consciousness* that is the source of all differentiated focal points of consciousness perceiving any world.

This chapter also discusses the basic reason for an impasse between science and spirituality. This impasse boils down to a fundamental disagreement in what we mean by *reality*. For science, *reality* is a perceivable world. For spirituality, *reality* is the source of any possible perceivable world and the source of the perceiving consciousness of that world.

The Gefter argument is based on two recent discoveries in modern physics (Susskind, 2008). The first discovery is the nature of dark energy and a cosmic horizon, and the second is the holographic principle. The discovery of dark energy is based on recent astronomical observations within the framework of relativity theory. The discovery of the holographic principle is based on mathematical consistency in the way quantum theory is unified with relativity theory, which is about how space-time geometry is quantized.

Astronomical observations show that the farther we look out in space, the faster the galaxies are moving away from us, as though everything in the universe repels everything else. This repulsive force is called the force of dark energy, and is understood as a kind of anti-gravity. In relativity theory, dark energy is understood as a cosmological constant.

The solutions to Einstein's equations with a positive cosmological constant describe an exponentially expanding space, called de Sitter space. The only way this kind of an exponentially expanding space can be understood is in terms of the expansion of space that expands at an accelerated rate relative to the central point of view of an observer. The farther out in space the observer looks, the faster the space expands away from the observer.

The exponential expansion of space results in a cosmic horizon surrounding the observer at the central point of view. At the observer's cosmic horizon, things appear to move away from the observer at the speed of light. Since nothing can travel faster than the speed of light, the cosmic horizon is as far out in space as the observer can see things in space. The observer's cosmic horizon is therefore a bounding surface of space fundamentally limiting the observer's observations of things in space.

A critical aspect of the cosmic horizon is its observer-dependence. In an exponentially expanding space with a positive cosmological constant, every observer is surrounded by its own cosmic horizon limiting its observations of things in space. Every observer is at the central point of view of its own observation-limiting, surrounding cosmic horizon.

Although the cosmic horizons of different observers can overlap with each other, the observer-dependence of the cosmic horizon tells us that every observer has its own cosmic horizon. By different observers, we can only refer to the differing focal points of consciousness that arise at the central point of view of different cosmic horizons.

The observation-limiting nature of the cosmic horizon implies symmetry breaking. The symmetry that is broken with a cosmic horizon is the symmetry of empty space. A positive cosmological constant breaks the symmetry of empty space by constructing a boundary in space surrounding the observer at the central point of view.

This symmetry breaking has profound implications in the way quantum theory is unified with relativity theory. The big problem is once we have a positive cosmological constant and every observer is surrounded by its own observation-limiting cosmic horizon, the symmetry of empty space is broken, and different observers no longer agree on the nature of the vacuum state. Since the observer's cosmic horizon is observer-dependent, different observers no longer agree on either the vacuum state or the spectrum of particle excitations from the vacuum.

The nature of this problem is called horizon complementarity (Susskind, 2008). Whenever an event horizon arises that limits the observations of an external accelerated observer, those observations no longer agree with the observations of a freely falling observer that falls freely through the event horizon. The external accelerated observer and the freely falling observer no longer agree on the nature of the vacuum state or the spectrum of particle excitations. The event horizon breaks the symmetry of empty space from the perspective of the external accelerated observer and so those observations do not agree with those of the freely falling observer. The external accelerated observer observes thermal particles of Hawking radiation, while the freely falling observer does not.

For the external accelerated observer, the event horizon is a *real* surface in space that has a temperature and radiates away *real* particles of Hawking radiation, while for the freely falling observer there are no particles of Hawking radiation and the event horizon is only an imaginary surface in space. Although the particles of Hawking radiation appear *real* for the external accelerated observer, they do not even exist for the freely falling observer, nor does the event horizon have a temperature.

If we define *real* as what is invariant and the same for all observers, then clearly, the thermal particles of Hawking radiation are not real, since the freely falling observer does not observe them. The particles of Hawking radiation only appear to be *real* and to exist for the external accelerated observer. The external accelerated observer and freely falling observer do not agree on the nature of the *reality* they observe, but since they can never communicate with each other or share information, there is no real disagreement. This inability to ever communicate with each other is called horizon complementarity.

This strange state of affairs has profound implications when we try to define what is ultimately real. The nature of ultimate reality is about the ultimate nature of existence. The bizarre conclusion of modern physics is that nothing observable is invariant and the same for all observers, and so *Nothing is ultimately real*, which is the same as to say *Nothing ultimately exists*. The problem we face is in understanding this *nothingness* as the ultimate nature of existence. The solution to this problem is in understanding ultimate reality not as *something* we can observe, but as the observing consciousness. If we understand the observing consciousness as *nothingness*, then the problem is solved.

We understand that ultimately only consciousness exists. To say this in a different way, the consciousness of the observer continues to exist even if the observer observes nothing. Ultimate reality is fundamentally about the ultimate nature of the observer's existence, but that ultimate existence can only be described as *nothingness*.

Horizon complementarity refers to the absolute impossibility of the external accelerated observer and the freely falling observer ever being able to share information with each other and compare their radically different observations. Since these two observers can never share any information about their radically different observations, there is no real disagreement in the sense of quantum complementarity. This is analogous to the situation in the double slit experiment, where there is no real disagreement when one observer measures a particle-like property while another observer measures a wave-like property.

The situation with a positive cosmological constant and an observer-dependent cosmic horizon is different than other event horizons, such as the event horizon of a black hole, since different cosmic horizons can overlap with each other in the sense of a Venn diagram and therefore it is possible that different observers can share information with each other to the degree their cosmic horizons overlap. Even so, the observer-dependent nature of each observer's cosmic horizon implies that there are observations that differ among differing observers and those differing observations need not agree. There will always be some information that the different observers do not share with each other.

As we look out across the observable universe, observers on the other side of the universe are looking back at us, but since our cosmic horizons only overlap to a limited degree, they do not see the same observable universe as we see. Is the observable universe we see any more real than the observable universe they see? If we define what is ultimately real as what is invariant and the same for all observers, then both our observations and their observations are ultimately unreal, since they are not the same. What appears to exist for us is not the same as what appears to exist for them. This isn't just the case for observers on the opposite side of the universe. This is also the case for observers that are apparently standing right next to each other. Since their central points of view are not exactly the same focal point, their cosmic horizons can only overlap to a limited extent.

The nature of the observer-dependent cosmic horizon can only take us so far in terms of understanding *ultimate reality* in the sense of what is invariant and is the same for all observers. To go further, it is necessary to discuss the holographic principle (Bousso, 2002).

The holographic principle is usually expressed as the covariant entropy bound. The idea of entropy arises from the idea of a bit of information that encodes information in a binary code of 1's and 0's. The amount of entropy that characterizes any region of space is the number of yes/no questions about that region of space that can be answered yes or no, like the question: is a particle located at this position in space at this moment of time?

The covariant entropy bound tells us there are a finite number of yes/no questions that can be asked about any finite region of space. This is what we expect if space-time geometry is quantized. In a quantized space-time geometry, there are a finite number of possible quantized position coordinates in any finite region of space that a particle can occupy at any quantized moment of time.

What is unexpected is that the total entropy of any region of space is not proportional to the three dimensional volume of that space, but is to the two dimensional surface area of a surface that bounds that region of space. If this bounding surface of space is a spherical surface of radius R, then the surface area is A = $4\pi R^2$. The total number of bits of information, n, that characterizes any finite region of space is specified in terms of the surface area, A, and the Planck area, $\ell^2 = \hbar G/c^3$, as n = $A/4\ell^2$.

The reason this result is unexpected is because particles occupy positions in space at moments of time. How then are we to interpret this result that all the bits of information answering all the yes/no questions *Is a particle located at this position in space at this moment of time* are encoded on the two dimensional bounding surface of that finite region of three dimensional space? The answer to this question is called a duality (Susskind, 2008).

The holographic principle is the most fundamental duality known about in physics. This is like the wave-particle duality of quantum theory, but defined at the fundamental level of quantized space-time geometry. When space-time geometry is quantized, there are a finite number of possible quantized position coordinates available for a particle to occupy in any finite region of space at any possible quantized moment of time. The strange way quantum theory is unified with relativity theory does not allow this quantized space-time geometry to be defined in that region of space. The space-time geometry is only definable on the bounding surface of that space.

Chapter 18. Science and Spirituality: A Perfect Standoff

The holographic principle is a duality that relates the bits of information encoded on a two dimensional bounding surface of space to the particles that appear to occupy position coordinates in three dimensional space at moments of time. The only way to interpret this duality is when we observe a particle at a position in space at some moment of time, that observation is like the projection of an image of the particle from a two dimensional screen to the central point of view of an observer (Smolin, 2001).

To make sense of this interpretation, we have to understand the bounding surface of space as a holographic screen and the projection of the image of something like a particle to the central point of view of the observer as a screen output, just like the kind of images we observe on a computer screen with each screen output. In the same sense, an animated sequence of screen outputs corresponds to a sequence of quantized moments of time.

The bits of information are encoded on the screen in a pixelated way with one bit of information encoded per pixel on the screen, giving rise to a finite number of possible quantized position coordinates in space that a particle can occupy at any possible moment of time. The observed motion of the particle then occurs over an animated sequence of screen outputs. The observation of the particle and its motion are specified by the way in which bits of information are encoded on the screen over a sequence of screen outputs.

In reality, the particle is no more real than an animated image projected from the screen to the point of view of the observer. How are we to understand the nature of the observer? The observer is only a focal point of consciousness that arises in relation to the screen.

How does the screen arise? A holographic screen can only be understood as an event horizon that arises from the point of view of an accelerated observer. Examples of how event horizons arise are black hole horizons that arise from the perspective of external accelerated observers due to the force of gravity, cosmic horizons that arise from the perspective of observers at the central point of view due to the force of dark energy, and Rindler horizons that arise from the point of view of an accelerated observer that follows an accelerated world-line through space-time geometry (Smolin, 2001).

In all these cases, the event horizon arises because the observer is in an accelerated frame of reference. An accelerated frame of reference is like a rocket-ship that accelerates through space due to the force of its thrusters. In the same sense that a rocket-ship must expend energy through the force of its thrusters as it accelerates through space, energy must be expended whenever an observer enters into an accelerated frame of reference.

The principle of equivalence tells us that the force of gravity an observer experiences is equivalent to an observer's accelerated frame of reference. There is no possible way an observer can distinguish between the force of gravity and an acceleration as long as we understand the observer to be a focal point of consciousness.

The way the fundamental forces of electromagnetism and the strong and weak nuclear forces are unified with gravity demonstrates that all the fundamental gauge forces are equivalent to an observer's accelerated frame of reference. We understand the unification in terms of the Kaluza-Klein mechanism (Susskind, 2008) and extra compactified dimensions of space. This tells us that gravity corresponds to accelerations through the usual three extended dimensions of space while the other gauge forces correspond to accelerations through an extra six compactified dimensions of space. Similarly, we understand the force of dark energy as the exponential expansion of space where space itself is accelerating. In this sense, all the fundamental forces are equivalent to an observer's accelerated frame of reference.

The observer's event horizon only arises if the observer enters into an accelerated frame of reference. In order for the observer's horizon to arise, energy must be expended. For a cosmic horizon to arise surrounding the observer at the central point of view, dark energy must be expended. We understand the expenditure of dark energy as the exponential expansion of space, which always expands relative to the observer's central point of view.

The holographic principle tells us the observer's horizon is a bounding surface of space that acts as a holographic screen and encodes bits of information. Everything the observer can observe in the space bounded by the screen is like the projection of images from the screen to the observer's central point of view. Those images are animated like the frames of a movie over a sequence of events that arise on the observer's accelerated world-line, where each event is like a screen output that projects images to the observer's central point of view.

The holographic principle is a duality translating between the way information is encoded on a bounding surface of space that acts as a holographic screen and the behavior of the particles observed in the space bounded by that surface. The observation of particles is like a projection of images from the screen to the central point of view of the observer. The observed motion of particles corresponds to the animation of the images over a sequence of screen outputs.

What are we to make of space-time geometry? Space-time geometry is a holographic projection from the bounding surface to the central point of view of the observer. The bounding surface acts as a holographic screen and with each screen output the observer makes observations of things in the space bounded by the screen. Each observation of something is a quantum state reduction that reduces the quantum state of the screen to an actual observable state. An observable state is defined by an actual configuration state of information defined on the screen while the quantum state of the screen is defined as a sum over all possible ways information can become encoded on the screen, which is a sum over all possible configuration states of information.

With the observation of things in space, not only are those things defined, but space-time geometry is also defined. Space-time geometry is defined with each screen output that reduces the quantum state of the screen to an actual configuration state of information.

The observer's holographic screen is an event horizon that only arises when the observer enters into an accelerated frame of reference. This happens whenever energy is expended, like a cosmic horizon that arises when dark energy is expended. We understand the observer is only a focal point of consciousness that arises in relation to its screen, like the observer at the central point of view that arises when a cosmic horizon arises. When energy is expended and the screen arises, the observer also arises.

Although it seems as though the observer follows an accelerated world-line through space-time geometry, the correct way to understand this state of affairs is in terms of the holographic screen that arises when energy is expended and the observer enters into an accelerated frame of reference. Space-time geometry, like everything else the observer can observe in its world, is a projection from the screen to the central point of view of the observer. Every event on the observer's accelerated world-line is another screen output. The key thing to understand is the observer and its screen arise together, but they can only arise when energy is expended in an accelerated frame of reference.

The big question is, from what do the observer and its screen arise? What is the nature of the ultimate reality from which an observer and its screen arise?

To answer this question we need to investigate how energy is expended. What gives rise to an accelerated frame of reference? We understand the observer to be a focal point of consciousness present at the central point of view of an accelerated frame of reference, while the observer's world is defined by the way information is encoded on the boundary of that reference frame. That boundary is an event horizon that acts as a holographic screen and projects images of the observer's world to the central point of view of the observer.

Gefter (2014) refers to this state of affairs as the "one-world-per-observer paradigm".

The key idea in the "one-world-per-observer paradigm" is that each observer at the central point of view has its own holographic screen, which defines everything the observer can possibly observe in its own world. Each observation reduces the quantum state of the screen to an actual configuration state of information defined on the screen, and is like a screen output. Each observational event on the observer's accelerated world-line through its projected space-time geometry is another screen output.

The holographic principle tells us the boundary is an event horizon that only arises if the observer is in an accelerated frame of reference which requires the expenditure of energy. What is the ultimate source of this energy?

Modern cosmology gives us the answer in terms of dark energy and the exponential expansion of space. Whenever dark energy is expended, space appears to expand at an accelerated rate relative to the observer's central point of view, and a surrounding cosmic horizon arises that limits the observer's observations of things in space.

If we take the big bang theory seriously, we understand that at the moment of creation of the observer's world, that world is about a Planck length in size, but that world then inflates in size because of an instability in dark energy. This instability in dark energy is like a process of burning that burns away the dark energy.

The expenditure of dark energy breaks the symmetry of empty space by constructing an observation-limiting cosmic

Chapter 18. Science and Spirituality: A Perfect Standoff

horizon that surrounds the observer at the central point of view. The instability in dark energy is like a process of burning that burns away the dark energy and *undoes* this broken symmetry. As the dark energy burns away to zero, the cosmic horizon inflates in size to infinity, and the symmetry is restored. We understand that this *undoing* of symmetry breaking is like a phase transition from a false vacuum state to a true vacuum state. As the phase transition occurs, dark energy burns away.

This burning away of dark energy explains the normal flow of energy in the observer's world in the sense of the second law of thermodynamics. This is easiest to understand in terms of a cosmological constant, Λ. Relativity theory (Bousso, 2002) tells us the size of the observer's cosmic horizon is related to the cosmological constant as $R^2/\ell^2 = 3/\Lambda$. The holographic principle tells us the absolute temperature of the cosmic horizon is related to its radius as $kT = \hbar c/2\pi R$. At the moment of creation, R is about equal to ℓ, Λ is about equal to 1, and the absolute temperature is about equal to 10^{32} degrees Kelvin. As the dark energy burns away, Λ decreases in value, R inflates in size, and the temperature cools. As Λ decreases to zero, R inflates to infinity, and the temperature cools to absolute zero.

This understanding is not only consistent with our understanding of the big bang event, but also with the current measured value of the cosmological constant, based on the rate at which distant galaxies are observed to accelerate away from us. The current measured value of Λ is about 10^{-123}, which corresponds to the size of the observable universe of about 15 billion light years.

The second law of thermodynamics simply says that heat tends to flow from a hotter object to a colder object because the hotter object radiates away more heat, which is thermal radiation. The instability in dark energy explains the second law as dark energy burns away, the observer's world inflates in size and cools in temperature, and heat tends to flow from hotter states of the observer's world to colder states of the observer's world.

The normal flow of energy through the observer's world simply reflects this normal flow of heat as the dark energy burns away and the observer's world inflates in size and cools. This normal flow of energy naturally arises in a thermal gradient. One of the mysteries of the second law is understanding the arrow of time, or how the normal course of time is related to this normal flow of energy. The burning away of dark energy explains this mystery. As far as the holographic principle goes, a thermal gradient is also a temporal gradient. The holographic principle reduces concepts of temperature, the normal flow of energy and the course of time to geometry, and so these concepts are intrinsically related to each other.

What are we to make of the expenditure of other forms of energy besides dark energy? Modern cosmology and physics again give the answer in terms of symmetry breaking. Observations indicate that the total energy of the observable universe is zero. This is possible in relativity theory since the negative potential energy of gravitational attraction can exactly cancel out the total amount of dark energy and any other forms of positive energy that arise from dark energy.

How do other forms of energy, like mass energy, arise from dark energy? The answer is symmetry breaking. As dark energy burns away, high energy photons are created, and these photons can create particle-antiparticle pairs, like proton-antiproton pairs. One of the mysteries of cosmology is why there are so many protons in the universe and so few antiprotons. Symmetry breaking gives the answer. At high energies, antiprotons can decay into electrons and protons into positrons, but there is a difference in the decay rates due to a broken symmetry, and so more antiprotons decay than protons. As the universe cools, the protons become stable, and so that is what we are left with. The expenditure of energy that characterizes the fundamental gauge forces, like electromagnetic energy in a living organism, or nuclear energy in a star, all arises from dark energy through a process of symmetry breaking, but all of this positive energy is exactly cancelled out by the negative potential energy of gravitational attraction.

The fact that the total energy of the observable universe exactly adds up to zero tells us something important. Since everything in the world is composed of energy and all of that energy ultimately adds up to zero, this tells us that everything is ultimately nothing.

Everything the observer can possibly observe in its world is like an image projected from its holographic screen to the observer's central point of view. All the bits of information that define the images are encoded on a two dimensional screen, but the projected images appear three dimensional since they're holographic. Those projected images are animated over a sequence of events in the flow of energy, just like the frames of a movie, and each observational event on the observer's world-line is another screen output.

The projected images are best understood in the sense of coherently organized forms of information, which can be understood in the sense of bound states of information that tend to hold together over a sequence of screen outputs. Coherent organization means forms tend to self-replicate their forms over a sequence of events and hold together as bound states of information. This animation of images over a sequence of events always arises in the flow of energy that characterizes the observer's accelerated world-line.

In relativity theory, we understand an observer's accelerated frame of reference as an accelerated world-line through space-time geometry. The holographic principle turns this understanding inside-out, since space-time geometry is a holographic projection from the observer's screen to the observer's central point of view. The observer only appears to follow an accelerated world-line through a space-time geometry that is projected from its holographic screen to the central point of view of the observer.

This gives us a natural explanation for the one-world-per-observer paradigm, but how do we understand a consensual reality shared by many observers? The answer is the holographic principle. Each observer's world is defined on its own holographic screen, but those bounding surfaces of space can overlap and share information. Many observers can share a consensual reality together to the degree their holographic screens overlap and share information.

The holographic principle also tells us that energy and information are really the same thing. Information is what energy looks like when observed at an instant of time. Each coherently organized form of information is composed of bits of information, and those forms of information are animated over a sequence of events. Energy is what a form of information looks like when that form is animated over a sequence of events. Information is a static concept while energy is a dynamic concept.

The equivalence of energy and information has a deep connection in quantum theory and in the way quantum theory is unified with relativity theory. When we speak of bits of information encoded on a holographic screen, we're speaking about the quantized bits of information that define everything observable in an observer's world. The observer's holographic screen is characterized by a quantum state describing all possible ways in which bits of information can become encoded on the screen. The quantum state of the screen defines everything the observer can possibly observe in its world. We can think of this quantum state as a sum over all possible configuration states of information, where a configuration state specifies a specific configuration in the way bits of information are encoded on the screen. A screen output must choose a specific configuration state from the quantum state when the observation of anything is observed. In quantum theory, this choice is called a quantum state reduction.

Quantum theory tells us that the observation of any observable thing by an observer implies an observer-observation-observable relationship, while any observation implies a choice as the quantum state of potentiality is reduced to an actual configuration state of information. In this sense, each screen output is a choice.

There is something very odd about quantum theory that is usually not discussed. Every quantum state reduction is a choice, which occurs at a decision point on the observer's world-line. At every decision point, the observer has a choice to make about what to observe in its world and which path to follow. Physicists have arbitrarily assumed that all choices are made randomly, in an unbiased way, but this assumption is only made since physicists want the laws of physics to have predictability. If choices are made in a biased way, then the laws of physics lose their predictability, and all bets are off, so to speak.

It's worth briefly reviewing of how choice operates in quantum theory. The quantum state can always be formalized as a sum over all possible paths that connect two points in some configuration space. For example, the configuration space could be space-time geometry, and then a path would be a world-line followed by an observer. In this sum over all paths formulation of the quantum state, we are instructed to sum over all possible paths in the configuration space, and then weight each path with a probability factor called the wave-function, $\psi = \exp(i\theta)$, where the phase angle θ is given in terms of the action S as $\theta = S/\hbar$.

The action is specified in terms of the geometrical length of the path. For example, for a world-line, the action is specified by the proper-time, which is defined in terms of the space-time metric. This is the case if there are 3+1 extended dimensions of space-time, but is also valid when there are

Chapter 18. Science and Spirituality: A Perfect Standoff

extra compactified dimensions, in which case the metric not only represents the force of gravity, but also represents all the gauge forces, like electromagnetism. With a cosmological constant, the metric also represents the force of dark energy. The metric is the natural way to unify all the fundamental forces.

Laws of physics are always expressed in terms of an action principle. Once we express S, we express the laws of physics, but the laws of physics only enter into the quantum state in terms of a probability factor ψ that gives weight to every possible path in the sum over all paths. The most likely path in the sense of quantum probability is the path of least action. Relativity theory tells us that the path of least action is like the shortest distance between two points in a curved space-time geometry, which is how we understand all of classical physics. The path of least action gives the maximal quantum probability, but this maximal likelihood is only meaningful if choices are made in an unbiased way.

What if there is bias in the way choices are made? Then, all bets are off, and the laws of physics lose their predictability. Physicists don't like that idea and so they've arbitrarily assumed only random choice is operative, but each of us knows that is not the way the world really works. Each of us is biased to choose what we like and to avoid what we don't like. This ability to choose what we like is the nature of our volition, or free will.

How are these choices made? The only possible answer is choices are made as the focus of attention of consciousness is focused on something. An observer chooses what it observes in its world with its focus of attention on that thing in its world. This makes perfectly good sense, since an observer is a focal point of consciousness. A focal point of consciousness is always at the central point of view of its own world, and that world is always defined on a holographic screen surrounding the central focal point. The observer expresses its volition or free will as it focuses its attention on something in its world.

There are two mysteries about the nature of consciousness that this explanation helps us understand. The first mystery is about how choices are made, which is the nature of free will. The answer is an observer chooses what it observes in its world as it focuses its attention on things in its world. The observer is always free to shift its focus of attention into a different direction and observe something different, thereby expressing its free will.

The second mystery is about how meaning is given to observations. The holographic principle tells us that the observation of anything occurs in a screen output but the nature of that thing is only a coherently organized form of information defined on the screen in terms of how bits of information are encoded on the screen. These forms of information are composed of bits of information encoded in a binary code of 1's and 0's.

How does a presence of consciousness give meaning to the forms of information it observes? The answer is, all meaning is given in an energetic context and this energetic context implies the expenditure of energy. The expenditure of energy is how a form of information is animated over a sequence of events. Only that animation of form creates the energetic context in which meaning is given to the form.

In emotional terms, or in terms of the animation of a body, the expenditure of energy creates the emotional context within which meaning is given. As is well known from the study of emotions (Damasio, 1999), all meaning is given in an emotional context. The expression of emotion is the expenditure of energy that animates the form of a body. Without this emotional expenditure of energy animating the form of the observer's body, the observer cannot give meaning to any form of information that it observes.

The solution to these two mysteries leads to an odd kind of emotional feedback loop. An observer chooses what it observes in its world with its focus of attention on things in that world, but the meaning it gives to those observations always occurs in an emotional context as energy is expended to animate a form of information in that world.

When we speak of an animated form of information in the observer's world, we are speaking about a coherently organized form of information that is displayed on the observer's holographic screen and self-replicated in form over a sequence of events.

Some of these observations are external sensory perceptions of the observer's world, which includes perceptions of the animated form of the observer's body, and some of these observations are internal perceptions that arise in mental imagination, like the perception of memories, emotions, thoughts, and other mentally constructed forms of information. The holographic principle tells us that there is really no difference in the nature of external and internal perceptions, since all animated forms of information are displayed on the observer's holographic screen. The observer is only a focal point of consciousness at the central point of view of the screen.

Whether the observed form of information is an external or internal perception, the observer can only give meaning to its perception in an emotional context. This gives rise to an emotional feedback loop that directs the observer's focus of attention on its world.

How can this emotional feedback loop direct the observer's focus of attention? There are two important ways this direction can occur. The first has to do with the alignment of the flow of energy. When the flow of energy comes into alignment, feelings of connection are perceived. When the flow of energy goes out of alignment, feelings of disconnection are perceived. Since feelings of connection feel "good" while feelings of disconnection feel "bad", the observer is naturally biased to choose feelings of connection and to avoid feelings of disconnection. That is how the observer expresses its volition by choosing what it likes and avoiding what it doesn't like. It likes what makes it "feel good", and doesn't like what makes it "feel bad".

This bias to "feel good" naturally directs the observer's focus of attention on its world in such a way as to keep the flow of energy through its world in alignment, thereby resulting in feelings of connection, which is the normal way in which the emotional feedback loop operates. This is normal since the natural way for energy to flow through that world when choices are made in an unbiased way is for the flow of energy to come into alignment.

Chapter 18. Science and Spirituality: A Perfect Standoff

This natural alignment in the flow of energy is a direct consequence of the principle of least action. Quantum theory tells us that as long as choices are made in an unbiased way, the motion of all things tends to follow the path of least action, and in the process, the flow of energy through all things tends to come into alignment.

The other way to understand the alignment of the flow of energy is in terms of the alignment of information. Bits of information encoded on a holographic screen are like spin variables that can only point up or down, but since the spin variables are entangled with each other like the eigenvalues of a matrix, they naturally tend to align together over the course of time, which is a sequence of screen outputs. The flow of energy through the observer's world tends to come into alignment as the bits of information align together.

The normal flow of energy can be understood in terms of the alignment in the flow of energy, which is understood in terms of the principle of least action, or in terms of the alignment of information, which is understood in terms of entanglement. Entanglement is operative over all of space. Events on opposite sides of the universe are related if the information for those events is entangled. Not as well appreciated is that entanglement is also operative over all of time. Events at the beginning of the universe are related to events now if the information for those events is entangled. In the sense of spirituality, prayer and devotion are a natural way of bringing oneself into alignment.

As long as a presence of consciousness makes its choices in its world by choosing "good" feelings of connection, the flow of energy in its world tends to remain in alignment, which is the normal way for energy to flow through its world. This kind of biased choice expresses the bias to "feel good", which leads to the "best of all possible worlds".

Problems can only arise in the observer's world when the observer becomes biased to choose feelings of disconnection, and the flow of energy goes out of alignment. Since feelings of disconnection feel "bad", why would the observer ever make these kinds of choices? Why would the observer ever express the bias to "feel bad"?

The answer to this question is called self-identification. Whenever an observer identifies itself with an animated form of information it perceives in its world, it naturally becomes biased to defend the survival of that form. The survival of a form of information is the self-replication of that form over a sequence of screen outputs.

Self-defensive expressions arise out of self-identification and result in feelings of disconnection. The observer focuses its attention on these self-defensive expressions due to its assumption that its existence depends on the survival of that form. This kind of emotional feedback loop is established because the observer really feels self-limited to the form of its body as it perceives the emotions expressed by its body that defend the survival of its body.

In the sense of the normal flow of energy, all self-defensive expressions are an interference with the normal flow of things that lead to "bad" feelings of disconnection, since the observer feels self-limited to the form of its body. Once self-identification occurs, the observer feels compelled to defend the survival of its body from all the threats posed by other things in the observer's world.

At the root of all self-defensive expressions is the fear of non-existence. This fearful feeling of self-limitation to the form of a body is the essence of all concepts of the self and the other. All concepts of self and other can only arise in an emotional context, and the expression of self-defensive emotions defines that context.

This self-defensive way of expending energy creates the emotional context within which an observer identifies itself with the form of its body and gives meaning to events in its world. The meaning the observer gives to the events arising within this emotional context then directs the observer's focus of attention on its world, which is a self-limited way of perceiving that world, as the observer identifies itself with the form of its body.

The principle of least action tells us that this self-defensive way of expending energy is always an interference with the normal flow of things. The normal alignment of the flow of energy and information creates feelings of connection, but this alignment is only possible when choices are made in an emotionally unbiased way. If choices are made in an unbiased way, the flow of energy tends to come into alignment. If choices are made in an emotionally biased way, the flow of energy tends to go out of alignment. The expression of biased emotions is directly related to biased choices, which are directly related to the bias in the focus of attention of consciousness. This bias arises because the observer identifies itself with an observable form of information. This bias always creates a disturbance in the normal flow of things. Self-defensive expressions express an emotional bias, which is always an interference with the normal flow of energy through the observer's world.

An observer expresses its volition and free will with its focus of attention. The observer is always free to redirect its focus of attention and make different choices. To the extent that bias arises in the way choices are made, that bias is the nature of individual volition. This bias is always emotional in nature, such as the self-defensive bias to defend the survival of one's body. The expression of an emotional bias is always an interference with the normal flow of energy that animates the behavior of all things.

The principle of least action tells us that when choices are made in an unbiased way, the motion of all things tends to follow the path of least action and the flow of energy tends to come into alignment. This alignment is the natural way for energy to flow through the observer's world. As long as there is no emotional bias in the way choices are made, the flow of energy tends to come into alignment, which is the natural way for energy to flow through the observer's world and to animate the behavior of all things, including the behavior of the observer's body.

This normal flow of things is what Wei Wu Wei (2003) means by *non-doing*. Everything one can do in the sense of individual volition is biased and is an interference with the normal flow of things, since biased behavior always expresses an emotional bias. When one is *non-doing*, one does nothing in an individual sense, and one no longer expresses any emotional bias. When one is *non-doing*, one allows all actions to play out in the normal way, and allows the flow of energy through all things to come into alignment, which is the normal way for energy to flow through all things in the observer's world.

This state of *non-doing* is a kind of *surrender*, as one stops fighting for the survival of one's self-identified form. This surrender is the willingness to no longer interfere with the normal flow of things. In this state of non-interference, there is no desire to fight against, control, defend, or hold onto anything. This willingness to surrender is inherently a detachment process, in which one is willing to let go of things. This willingness to *let go* and enter into a state of non-interference is the only way one can bring oneself into alignment with the normal flow of things, and stop identifying oneself with the form of one's body.

What is the real importance of this timeless wisdom of *non-doing*? Everywhere we look in the world, we see the fear of non-existence and the insanity of self-identification and self-defense express itself. This insanity is *Maya*, the emotional intelligence of fear run amok.

It is tempting to say that events in the world are unpredictable because of the overwhelming complexity of the world but that is not quite right. We could also say that events in the world are unpredictable because this complexity is not classically determined but arises in a quantum state, but that is also not quite right. Events in the world are unpredictable because of the emotionally biased nature of choice. Once the observer identifies itself with the form of its body, there is no predicting what the observer will choose with its emotionally biased focus of attention. Self-identification makes the emotional feedback loop biased in unpredictable ways.

The holographic principle tells us that the world an observer perceives is no more real than a virtual reality world displayed on a computer screen. Everything the observer can perceive in its world is no more real than an animated image projected from its screen to the observer's central point of view. This includes the animated form of the observer's body. The observer's self-identification with the animated form of its body only arises due to its emotional sense of being self-limited to the form of that body, which can only arise when the emotional feedback loop that directs the focus of attention becomes biased.

The holographic principle also tells us that the consensual reality shared by many observers is very much like an interactive computer network generated virtual reality world displayed on multiple computer screens and observed by many observers. Each observer observes its own world on its own holographic screen, but those screens can overlap and share information. Each observer makes choices in its own world with its own focus of attention on that world, but due to information sharing, the choices of other observers can have an effect on what each observer observes in its own world, which is the interactive nature of the network. The nature of the consensual reality is constructed out of all these interacting choices.

Each observer's world also shares in the flow of energy that energizes the entire network of screens. The consensual reality shared by many observers can share information to the degree their screens overlap, but each observer's holographic screen is ultimately defined by a cosmic horizon that arises from the expenditure of dark energy all the observers share together. All observers share in the normal flow of energy, and to the extent their choices are made in an unbiased way, share in the alignment of the flow of energy. Even when choices are made in an emotionally biased way, this interference only creates a localized disturbance in the normal flow of energy.

In spite of the complexity of this consensual reality, the nature of this kind of interactive virtual reality world is ultimately no more real than the perception of animated images projected from a digital computer screen to the central point of view of an observer.

The only way to define *ultimate reality* is in terms of what is invariant and the same for all observers. The holographic principle demonstrates the consensual reality shared by many observers is ultimately unreal, since whatever any individual observer observes will never be the same as what all other observers observe. Different observers can only share information to the extent their holographic screens overlap. Different observers will always observe different things, and so *Nothing is ultimately real*.

What is ultimately real? Is the observer real? If the observer isn't real, does the observer have an underlying reality? What is left when the observer's world disappears?

How can the observer's world disappear? The thing to be clear about is the observer's world can only appear from the central point of view of the observer. The observer's world can only appear when the observer expends energy and enters into an accelerated frame of reference, since that is the only way an event horizon can arise that surrounds the observer at the central point of view.

If the observer does not enter into an accelerated frame of reference and expend energy, then no event horizon arises, and the observer has no holographic screen that surrounds itself and defines everything in its world. If no energy is expended, then no information is encoded for the observer's world, and the observer's world must disappear.

What is left when the observer's world disappears? What is the nature of the underlying reality that remains when energy is no longer expended, when information is no longer encoded, and when the observer's world disappears?

There are many names for this underlying reality. It is sometimes called the void, empty space, or non-dual awareness. In the tradition of Shankara (Nisargadatta Maharaj, 1973), it is called Brahmanic consciousness. In physical terms, there is nothing in it, and so it is called the void. Probably the best name for it is undifferentiated consciousness. Since it is the source of consciousness and the source of energy, it is also called the Source.

The hardest thing to understand about the nature of this underlying reality is that the source of consciousness is undifferentiated consciousness. The consciousness that is characteristic of an observer and its world is a differentiated kind of consciousness, which can be called Atmanic consciousness. The differentiation of a point of consciousness from undifferentiated consciousness occurs at a focal point, which is the central point of view of a world holographically defined on a bounding surface of space. The differentiation process is the energetic construction of the boundary. The boundary is an event horizon that can only arise when energy is expended. The relation of a differentiated point of consciousness to the totality of undifferentiated consciousness is the relation of a focal point to the totality of an infinite empty space.

To be clear, this infinite empty space is an *empty space of potentiality*. The nature of this *space* is not defined by the boundary or the bounded space that arises inside the boundary. The bounding surface of space is a holographic screen that projects an observable space-time geometry to the central point of view of the observer. This observable space-time geometry is defined by properties like dimensionality and curvature, but these properties arise from the nature of the boundary, which is an event horizon that arises in an accelerated reference frame. A reference frame characterizes the horizon and the observer's world, but does not in any way characterize the empty space of potentiality within which the boundary arises. This empty space of potentiality cannot be characterized in terms of a dimensionality or any other physical properties. It is the source of all dimensions and physical characteristics.

The empty space of potentiality is the source of all dimensions, the source of all physical properties, the source of all space-time geometries, the source of all reference frames, the source of all energy, and the source of all information. The holographic principle explains how all these things arise in an accelerated frame of reference as energy is expended and the boundary of an event horizon arises. This boundary characterizes every aspect of the world bounded by that boundary, including its space-time geometry, but tells us nothing about the nature of the empty space of potentiality within which the boundary arises.

Another way to understand this *empty space of potentiality* is as a *void of undifferentiated consciousness*. As energy is expended in an accelerated reference frame and the boundary of an event horizon arises, a focal point of consciousness at the central point of view is differentiated from undifferentiated consciousness. The differentiation process is the construction of this boundary within empty space. The construction of the boundary requires the expenditure of energy. Empty space itself is the source of this energy, which we call dark energy and understand as the exponential expansion of space.

The expenditure of this energy is what causes a boundary to arise that surrounds the central focal point. This expenditure of energy is the nature of the differentiation process. Encoding of information for the observer's world only occurs when energy is expended.

The nature of an observer and its world is a constructed reality, which is to say that world is a bounded reality. The boundary is only constructed when energy is expended.

Information for the observer's world is only encoded on the boundary when energy is expended. The observer's world only appears when energy is expended. When energy is no longer expended, there is no longer a boundary, information is no longer encoded, and the observer's world disappears.

Disappearance of the observer's world always occurs relative to the central point of view of the observer.

What happens to the observer's consciousness when the observer's world disappears? What happens to this differentiated focal point of consciousness? The answer is the observer's consciousness is no longer differentiated from undifferentiated consciousness. The differentiated consciousness of the observer rejoins undifferentiated consciousness. This is often described as a dissolution, like a drop of water that dissolves back into the ocean. In the Tao this is referred to as *returning*, and in many religions as a *reunion*. In the sense of *Nirvana*, the final dissolution occurs when the *flame of life* is extinguished.

The underlying reality of undifferentiated consciousness is what is left when an observer and its world disappear from existence. It is not that the differentiated consciousness of an observer stops existing, but timelessly exists as undifferentiated consciousness. This experience of *timeless being* or *pure being* is often referred to as *truth-realization*.

Something remarkable happens after truth-realization that Plato calls *ascension*. After truth-realization, an observer observes its world again, but from an ascended level of consciousness, which is like a higher dimension. Ascension is often described in terms of an observer that observes the animated images of its world on a two dimensional screen from a higher dimension outside the screen. It is as though the observer has come out of its world, but it never really was in its world in the first place. There was only an illusion that the observer was a part of that world. That illusion is the nature of self-identification.

The observer is always present as a focal point of consciousness at the center of its world, while the animated images of that world are projected from a surrounding holographic screen to the observer. If the observer identifies itself with the form of an image that appears in its world, it seems as though the observer is a part of that world. This illusion comes to an end when the observer ascends to a higher level of consciousness and sees that these images are only displayed on a surrounding screen.

A truth-realized observer can turn off the expenditure of energy that constructs the boundary on which its world is displayed. When that expenditure of energy is turned off, the observer's world disappears and the observer's consciousness rejoins undifferentiated consciousness.

When energy is no longer expended, the observer is no longer in an accelerated frame of reference, the observer's holographic screen is no longer constructed, the observer's world disappears, and the observer is no longer present for that world. In relativity theory, a non-accelerated frame of reference is called a freely falling frame of reference.

A truth-realized observer can enter into an *ultimate freely falling frame of reference* at will, in which its world disappears, and only the *ultimate state of being* remains.

In some sense, the fear of non-being is the emotional barrier separating the *self-identified state of being* from the *ultimate state of being*, like a potential barrier separating a false vacuum state from the true vacuum state. In the same sense, the expression of the emotional energy of this fear of non-being is the energy that animates one's self-concept.

The expenditure of energy creates the emotional context within which the observer gives meaning to all the forms of information it perceives in its world. All worldly knowledge is a form of information, but meaning can only be given to knowledge in an emotional context. In the process of expressing self-limiting emotions and identifying itself with a form of information, the observer gives meaning to self-limiting emotional expressions that create the emotional context. The observer expresses emotions as it expends energy, and then gives meaning to its emotional expressions as they create the emotional context. Without that emotional context, all forms of self-knowledge become meaningless, and the observer becomes *knowledgeless*. A truth-realized observer *knows nothing* about itself, except for the timeless nature of its existence.

Without the expression of self-limiting emotions, no meaning can be given to the forms of information that create the observer's self-concept. Without the expenditure of energy that constructs a boundary upon which these forms of information are displayed, there is nothing to know. A truth-realized observer *sees everything*, since its consciousness is ascended, but *knows nothing*, since its consciousness is unbounded. The only true thing that a truth-realized observer can ever know about itself is *I Am*.

The standoff between science and spirituality is about what is meant by *reality*. For science, *reality* is perceivable reality, while for spirituality, *reality* is ultimate reality. This is the difference between *somethingness* and *nothingness*; the difference between what is perceivable and the perceiving consciousness; the difference between physical reality and spiritual reality; the difference between the manifested world and the unmanifested source of the world. There is a perfect standoff in this debate because when the term *reality* is used, science and spirituality are talking about different *things*.

So, is there a reason to prefer our perspective? We believe there is. By accepting that the individual consciousness is a microcosm of cosmic consciousness, it becomes possible to put forward an entire scientific framework for individual, organizational, national, and global transformation and peace as we have in this book. Diligent practice of the framework can lead to myriad of benefits in a variety of areas such as health and wellness, exemplary performance in all walks of life including business performance, better leadership decisions, and less discord and violence. We have explained that due to varying levels of consciousness of individuals, the benefits accrued will necessarily vary and for this reason, six sigma is the appropriate framework for analysis and not science.

References

[1] Bousso, Raphael, The Holographic Principle. http://arxiv.org/abs/hep-th/0203101, 2002.

[2] Damasio, Antonio, *The Feeling of What Happens*, Harcourt Brace, 1999.

[3] Gefter, Amanda, *Trespassing on Einstein's Lawn: A Father, a Daughter, the Meaning of Nothing, and the Beginning of Everything*, Random House, 2014.

[4] Kowall, James and Deshpande, Pradeep, Science and Spirituality: A Perfect Standoff. To be published in Scientific God Journal, 2014.

[5] Nisargadatta Maharaj, *I Am That*, The Acorn Press, 1973.
[6] Smolin, Lee, *Three Roads to Quantum Gravity*, Basic Books, 2001.
[7] Susskind, Leonard, *The Black Hole War*, Little, Brown and Company, 2008.
[8] Wei Wu Wei, *Fingers Pointing Towards the Moon*, Sentient Publications, 2003.

APPENDIX 1
Supplementary Information

A. Publications on Meditation

Table A.1. Articles on Meditation

No.	Authors	Journal	Outcome Investigated
1	Benson, H., et al.,	Nature, 295, 234 – 236, 21 Jan. 1982	Body Temperature Changes
2	Bhasin, M. K. et al.,	PLOS One, 8, 5, May 2013	Metabolism, Insulin Secretion, Inflammatory pathways
3	Boyers, J.	Forbes, May 30, 2013	Empathy
4	Condon, et al.,	Psychological Science, August 21, 2013.	Compassionate Response to Suffering
5	Deshpande, P. B., et al.,	Journal of Consciousness Exploration & Research, 5, 2, February 2014.	Materialization of Intentions
6	DeSteno, D.	New York Times, July 5, 2013	Compassionate Response to Suffering
7	George B.	HBR Blog, 10 March 10, 2014	Leadership
8	Fryer, B.	HBR Blog Network, September 18, 2013.	Compassionate Management
9	Lutz, et al.,	PNAS, 101, 46, November 16, 2004.	Gamma Wave Synchrony

10	Paul-Labrador, M., et al.	*Archives of Internal Medicine*, 166, 1218, 2006.	Metabolic Syndrome and Heart Disease
11	Paturel	NeurologyNow, August/September 2012.	Meditation as Medicine
12	Speca, M., et al.,	Journal of Biobehavioral Medicine,, Vol. 62 No. 5, 613-622, September 1, 2000.	Stress Reduction in Cancer Patients
13	Tang, Yi-Yuang, et al.,	PNAS, 110, 34, August 28, 2013.	Smoking Reduction
14	Ricard, Matthieu, Lutz, Antoine, David L. Richardson	Scientific American October 14, 2014	Neuroscience Reveals Secrets of Meditation's Benefits
14	Tang, Yi-Yuang, et al.,	PNAS, 109, 26, 10570-10574, 2012	White Matter Changes
15	Tang, Yi-Yuang, et al.,	PNAS, 106, 22, 8865-8870, 2009.	Central & Autonomic Nervous System
16	Tang, Yi-Yuang, et al.,	PNAS 104, 43, 17152-17156, 2007.	Attention and Self-Regulation
17	Wallace, R. K.	Science, Vol. 167, No. 3926, 1970.	Physiological effects
18	Walton, A. G.	Forbes, July 24, 2013.	Healthcare Costs, Student Performance

B. Famous Personalities Who Meditate (Source: Internet)

1. Prime Minister of India, Hon. Mr. Narendra Modi
2. Dr. John Hagelin, PhD Renowned Quantum Physicist
3. Marnie Abramson, Owner Tower Company Real Estate
4. Ramani Ayer, CEO Former Chairman & CEO, Hartford Financial Services Group
5. Marc Benioff, CEO Salesforce.com (Formerly at Oracle)
6. Roger Berkowitz, CEO Legal Sea Foods

7. Elizabeth Helen Blackburn, 2009 Nobel Prize Winner Medicine; Australian-American biological researcher at the University of California San Francisco
8. Brenda Boozer, Metropolitan Opera soloist
9. Larry Brilliant, Head Google Philanthropic Effort
10. Warren Buffett, Chairman, Berkshire Hathaway
11. Andrew Cherng, CEO Panda Express Founder
12. Ray Dalio, CEO, Bridgewater Associates, World's largest Hedge Fund
13. Larry Ellison, CEO Oracle
14. John Weber Denninger, Harvard University Medical School
15. Bill Ford, Chairman and CEO, Ford Motor Company
16. Ariana Huffington, President, and Editor-in-Chief of the Huffington Post Media Group
17. Bill Gates, Microsoft Founder and former Chairman
18. Bill George, Former CEO at Medtronic
19. Rick Goings, CEO Tupperware
20. Phil Jackson, NBA Coach
21. Steve Jobs, Apple Founder and former Chairman (deceased)
22. Brian David Josephson, Nobel Prize Winner; Welsh theoretical physicist and Professor Emeritus of Physics at the University of Cambridge
23. David Letterman. TV Talk show host
24. David Lynch, Film Director
25. Bob Shapiro, former Monsanto CEO
26. Renetta McCann, CEO Starcom North America
27. Mike Milken, Chairman Milken Institute
28. Rupert Murdoch, Australian/American business magnate
29. Steve Rubin, former Chairman & CEO, United Fuels International
30. Tony Schwartz, Founder & CEO, The Energy Project
31. Russell Simmons, Def Jam Founder
32. Nancy Solomwitz, CEO, Executive Management Associates
33. Robert Stiller, Founder, Green Mountain Coffee Roaster
34. Padmasree Warrior, CTO, Cisco Systems
35. Oprah Winfrey, CEO Harpo Productions Inc.

36. Tiger Woods, Professional Golfer
37. 36 Mark Zuckerberg, Facebook Founder and Chairman

C. Solicited Feedback on the Book

1. **Hon. Mr. Messiah Guevara Amasifuen**, Congressman of the Republic of Peru, Member of the Commission of Science, Technology and Innovation (Translation by Dr. Roberto Z. Tantalean).
   Professor Deshpande, a very well-known chemical engineer and scientist, offers us a book intended to provoke reflection on a topic of global interest, the existence or survival in a context of profound imbalances and threats which, ultimately, sets at risk life itself. The book is a conclusive work to demonstrate the enormous possibilities that emerge from a combination of what might be called philosophy of physics with the traditional Brahmanic. If the universe came out of nowhere at the moment of the Big Bang, it is thinkable that can also disappear into nothingness; then it is necessary to strengthen the human connection with the ultimate reality which is cosmic consciousness. This is a visionary book about the transformation that we hope occurs in the 21st century.

2. **Dr. Rebecca Martin,** Director, Institute for Integral Studies, Louisville, KY.
   This book brings a strong sense that the authors have loosed a tiger from its cage and then caught hold of its tail, taking the readers on a powerfully illuminating adventure! Their book integrates Science and the Great Teachings of the Ages to provide us with essential explanations, which support our attempts to achieve deeper understandings of our potential role in cosmic interaction. Readers are encouraged to pursue the intentional and awakened transformation of themselves and our world. Indeed, 'The Kingdom of Heaven lies within", and with the help of pioneers like Dr. Deshpande and Dr. Kowall, humanity may open 'Heaven's Gates'. To engage in coherence with Universal Consciousness is the 'Crowning of Humanity'

Many blessings on your work. We, the recipients of your illumined efforts, are most grateful.

3. **Dr. Kunwar P. Bhatnagar**, PhD, Professor Emeritus, Anatomical Sciences and Neurobiology, University of Louisville, Louisville, Kentucky

   In this latest expose on *Atman*-related sciences Drs. Pradeep Deshpande and Jim Kowall have taken bold steps toward understanding ***What The Ultimate Reality Is.*** Few would dare. Their new book deserves to be on one's Must Read list. The authors have added new beads of knowledge to their rosary of wisdom stepping towards the knowledge of the ***Inner Self***.

4. **Mr. Pradeep J. Mehta**, Former Vice President, Larson & Toubro, Ltd., Mumbai.

   The Book ("The Nature of Ultimate Reality and How it can Transform our World: Evidence from Modern Physics; Wisdom of YODA") will certainly generate genuine interest amongst Indians-Diaspora, whose emerging economy is on a threshold of "transformation" seeking an all pervasive, scientifically proved "mantra" like the one described by the authors.

5. **Dr. Babu Nahata**, PhD, Professor of Economics, University of Louisville.

   By exploring the mystery of both the external and the internal world, the authors not only provide an interesting new perspective of the true nature of the two worlds, but also articulate how both might be connected. By realizing that *nothingness* is the ultimate reality of both worlds, the authors propose meditation as a path that can truly transform the inner world.

6. **Dr. Mutyam V. Sharma**, FRCS, Diplomate of American Board of Emergency Medicine.

   Scriptures say we are what our thoughts are. Thoughts lead to words, words to action, action to habits, and habits to one's character. Superlatively analyzed, the book provides clues and ways to improve internal excellence.

7. **Dr. Roberto Z. Tantalean, PhD (University of Louisville).**
   It is not easy to relate Western and Eastern views as well Prof. Deshpande does on many important matters. I learned from him the fundamental concepts that helped me to understand the world as a unity not only based on the conventional physical laws but others that will intrigue the knowledge of modern society.

8. **Dr. Srinivas Yerrapragada, PhD** Former Post-Doctoral Scholar, University of Louisville
   A thought provoking root cause analysis of how an individual and society can methodically journey towards perfection. A must read for all professionals and non-professionals alike.

9. **Dr. Sandeep Dronawat, PhD (University of Louisville)**
   Dr. Deshpande is visionary in using data to raise human awareness of the Nature of Ultimate Reality. I have had the privilege of working under him and contribute to his research. His work has guided me in my success.

10. **Dmitry Orlov, General Manager, Bio-Well Company, St. Petersburg, Russia**
    If you don't know what is zero and eternity you can't count. If you want to freely surf the subtle interface of physical reality and consciousness world, you must read this book.

11. **Vibhu Sharma, Chairman and CEO, Ingenious, Inc. USA**.
    This book brings a unique perspective with a combination of real world industrial experience, as well as knowledge in quality improvement with a passion for excellence, both internal and external. Leveraging that knowledge combined with a higher level learning (i.e., Yoga), allows the authors to tie these two disparate worlds together. The overarching objective is to allow us to reach the pinnacle of performance and transform our world. Kudos to the authors for tackling this complex subject articulately.

About the Authors

Dr. Pradeep B. Deshpande is Professor Emeritus and a former Chair of the Department of Chemical Engineering at the University of Louisville; Visiting Professor of Management, Gatton College of Business & Economics, University of Kentucky; and President and Chief Executive Officer of Louisville-based Six Sigma and Advanced Controls, Inc. (SAC). Dr. Deshpande was among the first to introduce six sigma training in corporate India, and in engineering and MBA programs here, in Greece, and in India. He is an author or coauthor of six textbooks and over 100 refereed technical papers and presentations. He is a fellow of ISA, a recipient of numerous awards for research and teaching and is listed in *Who's Who in the World*. Dr. Deshpande has taught at the Indian Institutes of Technology in Kanpur and Madras, the University of Bombay, Department of Chemical Technology, and has spent a year while on sabbatical at India's National Chemical Laboratory in Pune.

Dr. James Paul Kowall obtained his PhD in Theoretical Physics at Brown University in 1980. He then served as a postdoctoral fellow at the University of California, Berkeley for two years before enrolling in medical school at the University of Miami graduating in 1984. He completed his residency in neurology at Stanford University during 1985-88 and served as a postdoctoral fellow there for a year. Jim is also board-certified in internal medicine and sleep disorders medicine. Subsequently, he was in private practice in Coos Bay Oregon until his retirement in 2008.

www.ingramcontent.com/pod-product-compliance
Lightning Source LLC
Chambersburg PA
CBHW060945230426
43665CB00015B/2074